Praise for
Splashes of Spirit ~ A Guide to Joy

"Have you ever read a book that made you feel better just reading it? Have you ever read a book that had the right words at the right time to boost your spirits and confidence? Have you ever read a book that kick-started you into action and reconnected you with your purpose? *Splashes of Spirit* is that book. Read it and reap."

-Sam Horn, CEO of the Intrigue Agency and
author of *Tongue Fu!*

"Jan's book is warmly accessible to anyone who knows they want to feel more joy in their life but doesn't know how to begin. She shares personal stories -- her own and others -- from a refreshing perspective: Not stories of those who know all the right answers, but rather from those who are asking all the right questions on the road to finding answers that are right for them."

-Susan Bliss Pearce, author of *OM-less?*
An Irreverent Guide to Knowing Grace

"Jan's God-given purpose is to SPLASH His love and joy onto everyone. Get ready: You're about to be SPLASHED!"
-Mickie Zada, CRW *(Cool Retired Woman),*
author of *Looking Behind Closed Doors*

"In a world of increasing stress, everyday bad news, and societal dysfunction, being joyful seems more difficult than ever. Well, help has arrived! *Splashes of Spirit ~ A Guide to Joy* provides us the tools to experience "joy" throughout our lives. It's more than an occasional emotion; it's a new mindset for a better life."

-Mason Harris, author of *The Chutzpah Advantage*

"Jan's *Guide to Joy* is a true road map for living life to its fullest. Her joy is poured onto every page, and her love of God and faith in God's plan for you is overflowing and infectious."

Dr. Michael Edwards, CEO of the Schuster Center,
author of *Through the Red Sea* and *Are You Essential?*

My dear friend, get ready to go on a joy journey with someone who not only embodies it brilliantly, but knows intuitively and skillfully how to guide you to your own. I have been blessed to work with Jan, and she is a light-bearer who infuses and inspires joy organically in those she teaches. This book is full of stories, inspiration, and guidance that will make your inner joy come alive! I'm so excited for you to experience the refreshing of your spirit, that I know is waiting for you in these pages. Enjoy!

-Michelle Cochran, Author of *Lead Like the Sun* and
CEO of SOAR Cafe & Farms

Splashes of Spirit

A Guide to Joy

Esther ~
I love your
joyful Spirit!
Jan

Jan Glowe-Janke

Jan Glowe-Janke

ISBN: 978-1-954693-00-5

First edition: 2021

FV-5

Cover Design by:
Kimberly Foreman
Foreman Design Group, LLC

Jan Glowe-Janke

This book is dedicated to

Sue Gabrielson, Mark Corless and Sam Horn

Jan Glowe-Janke

Contents

Endorsements   *i*

Foreword   *vii*

Dear Readers   *ix*

Listen to Your Guide So You Can Enjoy the Ride   *xi*

What is Joy?   *xvii*

Copy Genius   *xxii*

PART ONE: TAP into the TREASURE WITHIN

Chapter 1: Your Purpose   5

Chapter 2: Discover Your Purpose ~ A Guide   19

PART TWO: SPARK JOY ~ MIND, BODY and SPIRIT

Chapter 3: Stay C.A.L.M.   35

Chapter 4: Relax   47

Chapter 5: Refresh   59

Chapter 6: Renew   68

Chapter 7: Create S.P.A.C.E.   83

Chapter 8: Be the Star that You Are!   91

Chapter 9: Let Go   97

Chapter 10: Shake It Off   105

Chapter 11: Feed Your Faith   113

Chapter 12: Celebrate Resilience   129

PART THREE: JAZZ UP YOUR JOY
              with S.P.L.A.S.H. HABITS

Chapter 13: S   151

Chapter 14: P   157

Chapter 15: L   171

Chapter 16: A   179

Chapter 17: S   189

Chapter 18: H   203

Chapter 19: Holding My Purpose in My Heart   231

PART FOUR: CREATE YOUR JOY PLAN

Chapter 20: Keys to Jump Start Your Joy   241

Gratitude   251

Notes   257

Dive into Splash Calls   259

About the Author   261

Foreword

Joy. We all want it. We all seek it, and it's available to each one of us. But strangely, the best way to find joy isn't by chasing it head-on, but instead by embracing the One who brings joy from within even when everything from without is going wrong.

If you want more joy, and who doesn't, then you are in the right place. *Splashes of Spirit, A Guide to Joy* is the ideal guidebook to take you from here to there, and Jan Glowe-Janke is the perfect guide.

Like me, like you, Jan's life hasn't been always been easy, and like each of us, that twisty journey has taught her a lot of things along the way. And one of those lessons has been where and how to find joy. And it shows!

Jan is one of the most joyful people I've ever had the privilege of meeting, and as you get to know her through the pages of this book, I know you'll agree.

From tapping the treasure within, to sparking joy, to learning habits to train your mind and heart to always live from joy, this book will teach you, inspire you, and ignite a passion within you to live the purposeful, joyful, and impactful life that God has designed for you to live.

It's the adventure of a lifetime, and I can't wait for you to begin.

With you and for you,

Kim Avery

Author of the best-selling book, *The Prayer Powered Entrepreneur: 31 Days to Building Your Business with Less Stress and More Joy.*

My Dear Reader,

I'm delighted you're diving into this book — may it inspire you to nourish your joy! My hope is that you'll discover "gems"—takeaways — that you're excited to put into action. And I hope you'll begin to feel lighter and your struggles will seem less stressful as you connect to the joy within.

My prayer is that you'll be kind and gracious to yourself, that you'll give yourself permission to do those things that bring you joy — because that's when the best version of you will shine!

You do not have to be "religious" to benefit from this book. I speak in God-terms, and I believe that love, joy, peace and purpose are at the heart of all that is Divine. I invite you to read it through your lens; fit the concepts into your frame of reference. Joy is for everyone!

There is great power — and great joy — in discussion, repetition . . . and action. With that in mind, here are some suggestions to get the most out of this book.

1. *Read all the way through the book first to get an overview. Write your thoughts about the Points to Ponder at the end of each chapter.*

2. *Read "actively" with your pen in hand. Highlight parts that impact you. Note your thoughts in the margins.*

3. *As you read the book, you may want to keep a list of books, TED talks, podcasts, activities and websites for further study.*

4. *To multiply the joy, read the book with a friend or organize a small group. Talk about the questions at the end of each chapter in the first two sections.*

5. *In the SPLASH section, choose one joy habit each month – read that chapter every day, and act on it every day.*

6. *Refer to the Joy Plan framework in chapter 20 as you read each chapter. This free download is available on my website, https://janjanke.com*

7. *This is a book to read over and over again. Reference the book for quotes, Scripture, prayers and action steps – mine, and the ones you add.*

As you act on what you read, let your true spirit bubble up like a sparkling spring, splashing energy and life into everything you think, say and do. Relax and get ready . . . let's begin this journey to the joy that is within you.

Gratefully, joyfully yours,

Jan

Listen to Your Guide
So You Can Enjoy the Ride

My husband, Charlie and I were with a Vermont Bicycle Tour group, riding bicycles in the Canadian Rockies. As a side trip, we had the option to go white water rafting. Charlie jumped at the chance for another adventure. For me, the very thought of white water rafting churned up terror in my heart.

Are you adventurous like my husband? Or a scared-y cat like me?

At Charlie's coaxing I boarded the bus with twenty other brave souls. On the way to the Bow River, our guide casually said, "Normally at this time of year, the river is a level "3," but since we've had so much spring rain, it's up to a "4." I thought, "Let me off the bus. Now!"

Other buses were parked when we arrived at the drop-off point. I considered staying on the bus or even walking back to our cabin. But that was not to be. I was swept off the bus along with the crowd.

On the ground nearby was a pile of black wet suits, a pile of helmets and a pile of life jackets. We took turns scrounging around for ones that fit and donned our river gear.

The head guide gathered us all around him. He gave us instructions. If you have been white water rafting, you know the first three important instructions:

1. *Always listen to your guide for instructions*

2. *Stay calm*

3. *Relax and enjoy the ride*

I was swept up in the guide's enthusiasm about the river. His confidence was contagious.

We were prepared. We knew to listen to the guide, and he would instruct us every step, well, every paddle of the way. It was still scary, but I have to admit, I was feeling a bit exhilarated! There we were on that July day, standing on the banks of the beautiful Bow River. The sun was warm on my face, the morning air fresh and clean. I began to think, *"Maybe I really CAN relax and enjoy the ride."*

We were a parade of five yellow inflatable rafts, eight of us in each one, with a guide in the rear of each raft. Our raft was the second one to put in the river. We chanted playfully, "Stay in the boat! Stay in the boat!"

The first two minutes were smooth.

Then we came around a bend in the river . . . the raft in front of us was heading right into a rapids. We hung back and watched. I think we were holding our breath. Their guide was shouting instructions. They paddled furiously! They leaned together at their guide's command – and they made it through that rough water. They all stayed in the boat!

Mildly confident, we paddled forward. I thought, "If they can do it, so can we."

Within seconds, a *wall of water* appeared right in front of us. I am not kidding – it was a *wall of water* as high as a two-story building! The next thing I knew, I was under water, kicking and scrambling to get to the surface. Really, it was *that* fast! I saw the wall of water, then, in a heartbeat, I was in the depths of the river!

I surfaced, gasping for air. Our raft was within my sight. Charlie and another gal were the only ones still in the raft. I am always glad to see my husband, but never more than right then!

He had a look of relief on his face so I'm pretty sure he was glad to see me too. Charlie held out his paddle to me. I grabbed hold. He pulled me toward him and helped haul me back into the boat.

Then our guide appeared. He had been thrown overboard too! He quickly maneuvered our boat into shallow water. The others surfaced and scrambled back into the boat. Everyone was accounted for – except one. Hope was nowhere to be seen.

"She was probably swept down the river and picked up by the boat ahead of us," our guide said. We were all counting on that.

A few minutes later our parade of boats stopped, and we all gathered on the shore. The minute we laid eyes on Hope, all of us swarmed her. We were relieved she was safe and sound. She was happy to see us too, but she was clearly shaken. She tearfully told us, "I thought I was a goner! I've never been so terrified in all my life!"

The remainder of our time on the Bow River that day was beautiful and uneventful. Tidbits of the trip continued to surface in conversations every time we gathered for the rest of our week. We talked about our excitement (or apprehension for some of us!) at the beginning of the white water rafting adventure, the suddenness, the shock of the wall of water, and our fears when we were thrown overboard. We spoke with appreciation about how we helped each other get back in the boat.

We were all grateful for our guide. He had prepared us for the unexpected. When we encountered calamity, he stayed calm and confident. When our boat flipped, he was unfazed. In fact, he was exhilarated by the challenge. Beyond just enjoyment of the ride, our guide showed us that we really could embrace the adventure.

Rough waters . . . we've all been there.

And I'm betting you've had times when you felt like you were thrown overboard.

Have you felt suffocated by stress or drowned by doubts and fears?

Have you struggled through worry and anxiety?

We all have troubles and trials. In fact, Jesus tells us,

"...In the world you have tribulation and trials and distress
and frustration;
but be of good cheer
[take courage, be confident, certain, undaunted]!
For I have overcome the world.
[I have deprived it of power to harm you
and have conquered it for you.]"
John 16:33, Amplified Bible

Would you like to have someone guide you through rough waters? Do you want a guide to prepare you, to help you stay CALM and be of good cheer no matter the trials? I am offering to be your guide so you can relax and enjoy the ride.

Maybe you're thinking, "Jan, what qualifies you to be my guide? What qualifies you to write this book?" Good questions – I'm glad you asked!

I've encountered rough waters too, and truthfully, I have been thrown out of the boat many times.

➢ Divorce
➢ Months of vertigo
➢ Mom's diagnosis of pancreatic cancer, and Dad's death three months later
➢ My husband's diagnosis of aggressive cancer
➢ A business failure
➢ Having a dream that seemed way out of reach

Add to that my tendency to:

- ➢ Be a perfectionist – which means I procrastinate
- ➢ Second guess myself and worry
- ➢ Think "I don't know how"
- ➢ Feel "I'm not good enough"

Through times of uncertainty, self-doubts and fears, I have had wonderful friends, mentors, teachers and coaches who have set loving, gracious examples. They have shared their wisdom. They have supported and encouraged me. They have coached me so I could not only make it *through* rough waters, but come out better – stronger and wiser on the other side. As my gift to them, I am compelled to share the magnificent lessons I've learned with you. It is also my gift to God who put the desire on my heart to write a book about joy.

With your permission I will guide you to:

- ➢ Know and value who you truly are
- ➢ Discover and live your God-given purpose, your mission
- ➢ Stay C.A.L.M.
- ➢ Relax, refresh and renew your Spirit so you can be resilient
- ➢ Spark joy ~ mind, body and Spirit
- ➢ Jazz up your joy with a S.P.L.A.S.H.
- ➢ Create your own joy plan

I would be so honored and ecstatic to come alongside you and be your guide to more joy!

What is Joy?

Think about how you feel when your team wins, when you buy a new car or when you achieve a goal. You're excited and happy . . . maybe for a few minutes or even a few hours. Right?

That kind of happiness is *not* what I'm talking about here.

When I say *joy*, I am talking about a state of mind, an attitude. I use the words joy, happiness and positivity interchangeably, but please know I am referring to joy that is an inside-job, independent of circumstances. And it lasts.

I invite you into the kind of joy that makes us radiant, glowing from the inside. In Scripture John talks about streams of living water *flowing from within. "But those who drink the water I give will never be thirsty again. It becomes a fresh, bubbling spring within them, giving them eternal life"* (John 4:14 NLT).

Can you imagine being so grounded in joy that you could experience it no matter what is going on in your life, in your family, in your job, with your friends, in your health? It is possible. Joy is a mind-set and a heart-set. It is a choice.

Does that sound too pie-in-the-sky for you? Or do you think joy is for others but not for you? Maybe you're thinking, "I'm just naturally a glass-half-empty person," or "I'm too realistic to be positive," or "I'm too old to change."

But wait! I have great news for you! "Happiness is not the belief that we don't need to change. It is the realization that we can." That profound statement is from happiness expert, Shawn Achor, author of *The Happiness Advantage*. He also has a TEDx Talk; it's about how *we can train our brains to be more positive*. It is rich in research and wisdom. It's also really funny so I hope you'll treat yourself to Shawn Achor's TEDx Talk. [1]

How Do You Define Joy?

It is definitely not a one-size-fits-all.

Happiness expert, sociologist and author, Dr. Christine Carter, talks about joy as your sweet spot; it's when you experience a sense of ease and personal strength as you pursue meaning and fulfillment. [2]

Frank Mallinder, author of *Practical Wisdom, The Seeker's Guide to a Meaningful Life*, describes joy as feeling "peacefully supercharged."

Joyce Meyer, Christian speaker and author, defines joy as "calm delight—that steadfast sense of peace, pleasure and well-being we can only find through a personal relationship with God."

I asked friends what joy means to them. I'll share some of their responses:

➢ "Joy is a feeling of deep well-being and thankfulness."
➢ "I find joy with a sense of freedom."

➤ "It's being immersed in the moment."

Others said, "Joy is . . .

➤ contentment with a little awe thrown in."
➤ living my personal mission."
➤ living in God's tranquility."
➤ relaxing into who I really am authentically, feeling restful and calm."
➤ "Then there is profound joy, the moments you hold closest to your heart, the joy of being wrapped in the warm embrace of the ones you love the most – and you acknowledge that your life is amazing."

What is joy for you? Maybe it's "peace" or "harmony." However you define joy and however you experience it, that's just right for how you are created. Please know that joy is your birthright. Not only is it your birthright, the world needs your joy.

🐾🐾🐾🐾🐾🐾🐾

Let me share one of my Dad's favorite stories.

There are twin girls. One is a pessimist. Nothing is ever right; she is never happy. Her twin sister is an optimist. Everything is always right, always wonderful. She is joyful, all the time. The parents are baffled by how different the girls are so they take their daughters to a psychiatrist.

The psychiatrist takes the pessimistic twin to a room and opens the door. The room is filled with beautiful toys, games and stuffed animals. The little girl starts crying. The psychiatrist asks, "Why are you crying?"

The little pessimistic girl whines, "If I play with these toys, they will break!"

Next, the psychiatrist takes the optimistic twin to a different room and opens the door. The only thing in the room is a mountain of manure. The child squeals with delight, runs up that manure mountain and starts digging. The astonished psychiatrist says, "What are you doing?"

The little girl exclaims, "There's got to be a pony in here somewhere!"

You probably smiled at that story; maybe you laughed out loud.

Is there something inside you that wants to be more like that optimistic twin, someone who looks for the pony in the midst of . . . well, storms and trials? You can! As Shawn Achor says, we can train our brains to be more positive. He writes, "We are not our genes, our environments or our childhoods. At least, we don't have to be. By changing our habits, we can trump even our genes."

We can all be optimistic, glass-half-full people, if we want. If we want . . .

"You Gotta Wanna"

You've probably heard that joy is a choice. In the words of ten-year-old Amber, "You gotta wanna." Here's the story that prompted her wise words:

My fifth-grade students were deeply engaged in an art project. Bill Lundberg, Hillsdale College track coach, was teaching them how to make tennis ball puppets. His primary purpose for being with us was not just the art project. He was there to talk about the importance of positive attitude and desire.

As kids brought tennis balls to life with faces, capes and caps, Bill talked and my kids listened. Students talked and Bill listened. The conversation was sprinkled with playful laughter, and Bill took advantage of every teaching moment.

When everyone had finished creating a puppet, ten-year-old Amber paused, looked at Bill and said emphatically, "You gotta wanna!" What a beautiful summary of Bill's motivational message.

That's how it is with joy – you gotta wanna!

I'm guessing you are reading this book because you "wanna." You wanna have more joy in your heart and in your life. Congratulations for taking responsibility for your joy ~ I'm delighted you are here!

*Before we dive into habits
that train our brains to be more positive,
let's talk about people who show us what living in
joy looks like.*

Jan Glowe-Janke

Copy Genius

I heard it first from Dr. Mike Edwards. [3] "Copy genius," he said. I was with dentists from around the country as a coach at a "Live Your Dream" Retreat.

Mike explained, "When you see someone getting the results you want, learn from that person; do what they did. Read the same things they read; take the classes they took. When you walk in their shoes, walk the same path, you will come to an understanding and a shared philosophy; then you can enjoy a shared success."

Who is Genius at Joy?

> ➢ The saints and mystics. They show us how to love and live passionately and joyfully – in the midst of suffering and in the midst of our own human frailty.

> ➢ Modern-day, real-life saints and mystics – people like you and me!

> ➢ People who live in the Blue Zones, those areas in the world where people live longer, healthier, happier lives.

Lessons from the Saints and Mystics

Tessa Bielecki studies the saints and mystics. I love her CD set, *Wild at Heart*. I encourage you to listen for yourself – it will refresh and renew your Spirit.

I'll admit I had to look up definitions of saints and mystics. A saint is "a person of great holiness (dedicated and devoted to the service of God), virtue and benevolence." A mystic is "a person who claims to attain or believes in the possibility of attaining insights into the mysteries transcending ordinary human knowledge by direct communication with the Divine."

When I first read those definitions, I thought, "Way too lofty for me!" Is that your thought too? But wait! There is hope for us . . . really. Everybody can be a mystic. Every person can have direct communication with God.

I'm excited to share highlights of Tessa's work with you:

- ➢ Saints and mystics live with passion.
- ➢ They are wild about God.
- ➢ They are wild about life, suffering and death.
- ➢ They have passion for people, prayer and service.
- ➢ They graciously accept human weakness, their own and others.
- ➢ They live with hope and laughter.
- ➢ They are resilient.

"Mystics love the materiality of the universe," Tessa says. St. Columba loved his horse. Joan of Arc loved her horse too. Other saints loved asparagus, chess, and music halls. St. Bridgette loved beer. That makes saints seem pretty real, doesn't it?

And there's more . . . Tessa tells us these saints had a wild sense of humor. Not just quiet joy, but uproarious! She says:

"They take God alone so seriously that they can take everything else, especially themselves, lightheartedly."

We have much to learn from these "daring holy people."

They were daring in their choice to live and love extravagantly – in spite of suffering.

Saints are daring in choosing to *take heart* and *be of good cheer*, to live with joy, uproarious joy!

That's my prayer for us too:

"God, help us choose to take heart and be of good cheer, even in the midst of suffering. Help us to be like the saints who take you alone so seriously that we can take everything else, especially ourselves, lightheartedly."

Much has been written about the saints and mystics of ages past. Let's learn from them *and* from modern-day saints and mystics, those who live among us.

You and I know people who are devoted to God – real-live saints (even though they are not officially canonized). We know mystics among us. We have friends and family who love really well, people who have beyond-this-world insight and understanding which comes from their direct communication with God. Isn't it heartwarming (and maybe a little scary and a lot humbling) to know that you and I might be considered saints and mystics too?

I am especially excited to introduce you in the pages of this book to the saints who enrich my life. They will warm your heart and enrich your life too.

Lessons from the Blue Zones

First, you need to know Blue Zones have nothing to do with politics! The Blue Zones I'm talking about are those areas in the world where people live longer.

Dan Buettner interviewed dozens of centenarians in these identified areas and methodically studied each of the local lifestyles, habits and practices. Dan and his team discovered common ingredients of living longer. We can learn a lot about living longer, healthier, happier lives from his book, *The Blue Zones, 9 Lessons for Living Longer from the People Who've Lived the Longest.*

I love that it's not just a scientific book about living longer; it's personal; we get to know these people who live active, fulfilling lives – into their 90s and 100s. Through Dan's interviews with centenarians, we get the true flavor of their lifestyle, diet and outlook, including ways to avoid depression and keep our minds sharper.

We'll learn lifestyle lessons from people in the Blue Zones regarding how they:

➤ Have a strong sense of purpose

➤ Have moderate, regular physical activity

➤ Reduce stress (take time to "downshift")

➤ Have faith

➤ Have strong social connections

Throughout the book we'll *COPY THE JOY GENIUS* of saints and mystics of ages past, modern-day saints and mystics and people in the Blue Zones.

As you read, your own definition of joy will become clearer, and you will see what you can do to actually experience more joy.

"We are stars wrapped in skin. The light you are seeking has always been within."

-Rumi

Jan Glowe-Janke

Splashes of Spirit

A Guide to Joy

Jan Glowe-Janke

Part One

Tap into
the Treasure Within

Jan Glowe-Janke

Chapter 1

Your Purpose

"If you seek happiness you will not find it. But if you seek your God-given purpose, happiness will find you."
-Pastor Tony Evans

The Truth about You

I am going to tell you the truth about you. It is a most magnificent truth . . .

You are extraordinary!

Of the more than 100 billion people who have ever walked the face of this earth,

➢ You are one of a kind.

➢ You are a priceless treasure.

➢ You are God's masterpiece.

➢ You are created in His image.

➢ God created you on purpose, for a purpose.

Please consider saying each sentence out loud, personalizing it:

> I am one of a kind.

> I am a priceless treasure.

> I am God's masterpiece.

> I am created in His image.

> God created me on purpose, for a purpose.

Soak those Truths into your soul. Bask in those thoughts. Treasure them in your heart. Say those sentences out loud over and over again. Say them like you mean it. Slowly and deliberately repeat the sentences until you know the Truth. Keep speaking them until you begin to believe it. Put your hand on your heart, feel God's love, and mindfully say each sentence.

This is not bragging, not boasting. You are simply stating the Truth, God's Truth about you.

If you still have trouble thinking and saying these Truths, you could try it another way. Start each sentence with a "thank you" to God.

> "Thank you, God, that I am a priceless treasure in your eyes."

> "Thank you, God, that I am your masterpiece."

> "Thank you, God, that you created me on purpose, for a purpose."

You are extraordinary!
God created you on purpose, for a purpose.

You Are Extraordinary

The Truths you just read are lifted directly from Scripture.

"For we are God's workmanship, created in Christ Jesus to do good works, which God prepared in advance for us to do."

Ephesians 2:10 NIV

Workmanship implies work of art. We are God's work of art – his poem, his song – his masterpiece! Please pause and meditate on that.

When we are doing the good works we were created to do, someone will be helped; one person or many people will be served.

The "we" part of this Scripture is significant. In Pastor Phil Stout's "Time Alone with God" (TAWG, 3 September 2019) daily devotional, he writes, "Abundance is not personal. It's communal. God did not want a person to abound. He wanted a people to abound. It's not about me. It's about 'us', and 'us' includes all who are created in the image of God."

Furthermore, "The purpose of your life fits into a much larger, cosmic purpose that God has designed for eternity," writes Rick Warren, author of *The Purpose-Driven Life*. Isn't that incredibly profound? I am filled with awe and wonder when I think that each of us is God's masterpiece and that our purpose is part of God's grand plan for now and for eternity.

Knowing our individual, God-given purpose is essential – for the sake of our own joy and for the part we play in the grand scheme of it all.

YOU are God's masterpiece.
YOUR PURPOSE is part of God's grand plan.

What I Didn't Know

Did you know that you are created on purpose for a purpose? I am honored to tell you so. It truly puts us on holy ground.

I also have to be honest and tell you that I didn't know it – for a very long time. I was nearly fifty years old when I first heard that message.

Though I didn't know I was created on purpose for a purpose, I did know that I wanted to be a teacher since I was in third grade. When I was in seventh grade, I loved my English teacher, Mrs. Densmore, and I knew I was going to be a junior high English teacher. Not just wanted to be, but *knew I was going to be* a junior high English teacher! I was like a horse with blinders on, looking at only one goal.

Because I was focused on one goal, I went to college, took all the required classes, even the ones I thought were a waste of time, and graduated. When I was hired for a fifth-grade teaching position my second year out of college, I was in heaven! It didn't matter that my classroom was in an old chicken coop (that's the truth!) and every time it rained, the room flooded, and when I was working in the evenings, mice kept me company. The only thing that mattered to me was the joy of teaching!

I loved my upper elementary students, and I knew I was making a difference in their lives. I could hardly wait to go to school every day. Joy, energy and fulfillment were precious, priceless gifts that students and teaching gave me.

I didn't know I was created for a purpose. But I was instinctively following my passion.

Life became even sweeter five years later when I was hired as a junior high English teacher.

Fast forward through fifteen wonderful years.

Then, life took a twist. I left my dream job of teaching middle school English to become a counselor in the high school. Are you wondering, "Why would you leave a job you loved, one that you wanted all your life?" I asked myself the same question when the high school principal invited me to consider the counseling position. Had my life been normal, I never would have given that high school counseling position a second thought.

But my life was not normal. Life as I knew it had come to an abrupt halt.

My mom had been diagnosed with pancreatic cancer. Just three months after her diagnosis, my dad succumbed to chronic leukemia. I was so focused on taking care of

Mom that I didn't really grieve the loss of my dad. After his funeral, Mom came to live with my husband and me.

I accepted the counseling job so I could have more time with Mom and not have the nightly work that teaching English required.

Mom lived pretty well four years beyond her diagnosis. She actually was a kind of miracle because most people don't live even a year with pancreatic cancer. In the last few months of her life, she became so thin, weak and weary. Mom died in May, a few months after I started the counseling job.

The losses piled up. They paralyzed me. I was in a heavy, dark tunnel I couldn't crawl out of.

I was no longer a daughter. I was no longer a teacher.

I lost my joy. Lost my energy. Lost my passion to be around people. Life was a struggle.

Have you ever felt like that? Life was a struggle?

Thankfully, that was not the end of my story.

> ### If you're struggling now,
> ### it's not the end of your story either.

One of my favorite quotes is Gracie Allen's, *"Never place a period where God has placed a comma."*

That quote implies that it's all part of the learning, growing process. God can use everything for good, every experience we have and every emotion we feel. Life is more – we are more – than what is happening *to* us.

Here's what I didn't know: I am God's child. He created me. He loves me way more than I can imagine. He has a purpose and good plans for me. I don't have to *do* anything to earn his love and favor. The most important "job" he gives me is to love him with all my heart and soul and mind. My second most important "job" is to love others and love myself.

What I Know Now

My identity was totally tied up in my job. "A teacher." That's who I thought I was. "A daughter." Also, who I thought I was.

It wasn't. It isn't. I am so much more than what I do, more than any job and any role.

And so are you.

> *"Life can only be understood backwards,*
> *but it must be lived forward."*
> -Soren Kierkegaard

Looking backwards has helped me understand and appreciate so much. Look back with me.

Even though it didn't feel like it, I must have been living forward on those dark, difficult days and months, even years, after Mom's death.

My good friend, Delores, invited me to her church. The worship and the sermons touched my heart and soothed my soul. I loved the learning. I wanted to be there, to be around the many people who radiated joy. I didn't want to miss church.

Shortly before I retired from education, Pastor Ron delivered an inspiring sermon about mission statements. He talked about how important it is to know your purpose and to have a written personal mission statement. He said, "If you think you are going to retire and read junky novels, you probably want to think again."

Yikes! I felt like he was talking right to me. And I wanted to tell him that the books I was stockpiling to read were not junky. Even though I was a bit offended, his sermon really got my attention. It put me on a mission to figure out my personal mission statement. I read *The Path* by Laurie Beth Jones, and I diligently did all the exercises in the book. I journaled and wrote and obsessively kept working at it, but I still couldn't get my mission statement nailed down.

🐾🐾🐾🐾🐾🐾🐾

A year after I retired, I joined a network marketing company. I met Mickie. We worked together a lot on the phone, and we communicated through emails. I noticed a signature line on one of her emails, *Be Yourself Now Coaching.* I called and asked her about it. She said, "I coach a class, and I help people write their mission statements." As you probably guessed, I signed up on the spot!

In class on the phone one evening (it was before Zoom), I read aloud a paragraph I'd written. When I read, "I am a bubbling-over fountain of God's love and joy splashing onto everyone," Mickie jubilantly exclaimed, "Jan, that's it

– That's your mission statement! It's who you are at your core."

It took my coach to shine a light on what I couldn't see.

Consider These Truths

➢ We each have a light within us. (Matthew 5:14)

➢ We shine our light for God's glory. (Matthew 5:16)

➢ Our good works flow out of our relationship with God. (John 4:14)

➢ God created us to serve others, and in the serving, find significance, fulfillment, and meaning. (Ephesians 2:10 and John 10:10)

➢ It's all a process of learning and growing. And every day is a fresh start. (Lamentations 3: 22,23)

> *One thing I know for sure: True joy*
> *is knowing who you are and*
> *becoming who you are created to be.*

Purpose – or Something Else – Drives Your Life

You may be wondering, "Why is it so important to know our purpose?"

Pastor Rick Warren addresses that question in his book, *The Purpose-Driven Life.* He writes, "Everyone's life is driven by something . . . What is the driving force in your life? Right now, you may be driven by a problem, a pressure, or a deadline. You may be driven by a painful memory, a haunting fear, or an unconscious belief. There are hundreds of circumstances, values and emotions that can drive your life." [4]

He names five of the most common life-driving forces:

➢ Guilt

➢ Resentment and anger

➢ Fear

➢ Materialism

➢ Need for approval

I can look back on my life and readily see times when fear, anger and the need for approval were the driving forces of my life. It wasn't pretty. It wasn't fruitful. It certainly wasn't fulfilling.

Rick Warren writes, "A life driven by guilt, anger, fear, materialism or the need for approval leads to unused potential, unnecessary stress and an unfulfilled life." I can relate, and maybe you can too. Pastor Warren continues, "Nothing matters more than knowing God's purposes for your life, and nothing can compensate for not knowing them – not success, wealth, fame or pleasure." [5]

Knowing Your Purpose
Has a Plethora of Perks

Knowing your God-given purpose has everything to do with joy. "Finding meaning and purpose in life is the key component to being happy," states happiness expert and author, Christine Carter, Ph.D. [6]

Did you catch that? Meaning and purpose is *the key* component, not just one component, to being happy.

> ### *True JOY is knowing who you are and becoming who you are created to be.*

Experts agree that knowing your purpose reduces stress, helps you focus, simplifies your decisions and gives meaning to your life. Your mission statement is your North Star in all life's storms and troubles, in all seasons of your life. Sure wish I'd known my mission statement earlier in my life. The good news is that it's never too late to discover your purpose.

My personal mission statement is to Splash God's love and joy onto everyone. That discovery has turned my retirement into re-FIRE-ment!

My professional mission statement flows out of my personal mission. The purpose for my coaching and speaking business is to guide others to their joy.

Discovering my purpose and being intentional about aligning my life with it has given me more confidence and more joy. When I focus on God's plan for my life – splashing his love and joy -- my fears take a back seat. When I'm thinking about splashing, I'm not second-guessing myself.

The deepest desire of my heart is to guide you to discover your purpose so you too can experience the joy and the plethora of perks of knowing and living your purpose.

Knowing your purpose and aligning your life with it can have the utmost impact on your deepest fulfillment and your most sustainable joy. It will also have great impact on the difference you make in the world.

"What on earth am I here for?" Pastor Rick Warren says that's life's most important question.

Discovering your purpose for your life on earth is some of the most important and impactful personal growth work you will ever do because it is the foundation of everything you think, say and do. It is *a process* that requires reflection, prayer and patience.

Your Journey ~ What Do You Know?

If you've visited a big park or forest area intending to hike, the first thing you probably do is look for a posted map to give you the lay of the land. Then you look for the arrow pointing to a spot labeled, "You are here."

I don't have the advantage of knowing exactly where you are on life's journey, but I'm glad you're here – on this earth and reading this book. The information you are about to read may be new to you, or it could be a reminder.

Maybe you have the desire to discover your purpose, your mission, because you want more joy. Or perhaps you've already written your mission statement, and it's tucked in a drawer or in the back of your mind. Maybe you are just curious about the whole concept of a life's purpose. Or perhaps you have a clear sense of purpose, and you want to live it more consistently.

Maybe you're at a place where you feel like there's something missing, in your heart or in your life. Maybe you're busy, but you don't feel productive. Maybe you're facing a transition – kids leaving home, retirement, divorce, illness or aging issues.

Wherever you are on this journey, you have a light to shine. I want to encourage you and guide you to discover your God-given purpose. When you bring your extraordinary self to the surface, your light will shine – and the world needs your light!

Points to Ponder

1. What are your gems from Your Purpose chapter? (What did you learn? What are your important take-aways?)

2. What might be obstacles to discovering and/or writing your mission statement?

3. What perks make you want to discover and write your mission statement?

Chapter 2

Discover Your Purpose ~ A Guide

Joyce Meyer is a Bible teacher, speaker and author. At one of her conferences she said, "Maybe you came here for a word from God. Well, here it is: "Love God. Love others." That's Joyce – She gets right to the point. She concisely captured God's purpose for all of us.

Jesus said, *"Love the Lord your God with all your heart and with all your soul and with all your mind. This is the first and greatest commandment. And the second is like it: Love your neighbor as yourself. All the Law and the Prophets hang on these two commandments" (Matthew 22: 37 – 40 NIV).*

Beyond that very tall order to love God, love our neighbors and love ourselves, God created each of us for a specific purpose.

"Each of us is an original."
Galatians 5:26 MSG

What on Earth Am I Here For?

Kelly, Kim, Rebecca, Glenn and Mandie know the answer to that question. They know God's first and greatest commandment – they are put here to love God, love their neighbors and love themselves.

Each of them has also done the work to discover the purpose for which they were individually created. I am proud and excited to share their mission statements with you:

- ❖ God put Kelly on this earth to spark confidence.
- ❖ Kim's mission is to heal and revive the spirits of others.
- ❖ God put Rebecca on this earth to actively amplify his mercy.
- ❖ Glenn's mission is to inspire hope.
- ❖ Mandie's mission is to craft opportunities for authenticity for dreamers and do-ers.

Kelly, Kim, Rebecca, Glenn and Mandie participated in my workshop, "What on Earth Am I Here For?" They were whole-hearted in the process of writing their mission statements, a process that requires a lot of time and energy, prayer, listening and reflection. It's inside-out work, not something that's really taught or valued in our culture. It's a process that takes patience and persistence.

"Make a careful exploration of who you are and the work you have been given, and then sink yourself into that . . ."
Galatians 6: 4 MSG

Scripture directs us to discover and live our God-given purpose. In this chapter we'll do exactly that: We'll make a "careful exploration of who you are and the work you have been given." It's a big step toward your true joy.

Let's approach this project with a relaxed, joyful, expectant spirit. Please do whatever you need to do to make it enjoyable. Play your favorite music, light a candle, or read, discuss and do the exercises with a friend. If you're working on one question, and no answers come to you, that's okay. Just go on to the next one. Ideas will probably pop into your head and heart when you least expect them, when you quit striving. Take breaks when you need to. Put a smile on your face, and let's get started.

Your God-Given Purpose is Your Mission

Think of your God-given purpose as your mission for this life. Your mission is the task, the assignment, God has given you.

> *Your mission statement, your statement of purpose,*
> *is a written, concise statement*
> *that captures what on earth you are here for.*

Elements of Your Mission Statement

It's Uniquely Yours

It's a sentence you can say in a breath, it's uniquely yours, and it rocks you out of bed in the morning. It excites you and energizes you. At the same time, it fills you with a peace, a knowing. You remember it, and you say it out loud. It's imprinted on your brain and on your heart.

It's All about Serving

Your mission is about serving. It requires action. When you live your mission, someone will be helped, encouraged, loved or healed. As you serve, your life and others' lives will be better.

It's All-Encompassing

Think of your mission as an umbrella. It covers all areas of your life, all the hats you wear, all the roles you play. I'll use mine as an example: Splash his love and joy onto everyone – in all my relationships, in my jobs, in my responsibilities, and even when I am just out and about.

It's a Life-Time Pursuit

Just as your mission statement is an umbrella statement covering all areas of your life; it covers all seasons of your life. The "how" you live your mission may be different at various stages, but the purpose stays the same. It is your North Star throughout your life.

It's God-Sized

Pastor Ron said, "If you write your mission statement, and it's something you can do on your own, it isn't your mission." Actually, that's kind of a relief! Here's how that works for me: My mission is to Splash God's love and joy onto everyone. The "onto everyone" is the God-sized part.

There's no way I can (or would want to) do that on my own. Quite honestly, I would pick and choose the people I like and enjoy to splash on, but God is very clear that I'm to splash His love and joy on *every*one. He designed us to need Him, to rely on him to fulfill the task he's put us on this earth to do.

Put on Your "Whatever It Takes" Spirit

I must be very honest with you. Writing my mission statement was often hard work, and it took a long time. I knew instinctively that it was very important "work," a project that would have great impact on me, on my life and on others. I thought I could do it on my own.

I couldn't.

Pastor Ron had recommended *The Path* by Laurie Beth Jones. I read it all, many times. I did all the exercises in it. I read and journaled. I prayed. Others prayed for me. I wrote rough draft after rough draft, but nothing was a fit. And I was very frustrated.

Finally, I hired a coach. That made all the difference. Mickie, my coach, helped me "get it." It took my coach to shine a light on what I couldn't see. Oh, the joy of knowing, really knowing, why God put me on this earth! It was an exciting, life-changing accomplishment and discovery. I felt like doing cartwheels and backflips!

I tell you my mission statement experience *not* to discourage you, but to prepare you. I tell you in hopes that my story will help you patiently trust the process and give you hope. I pray that you truly "wanna" discover your mission and for God to give you a "whatever it takes" Spirit. I am praying for you to get crystal clear about your purpose for this life.

> *Discovering your God-given purpose is the first key to your true joy.*

A 7-Step Guide to Discover Your Purpose and Develop Your Mission Statement

This mission statement writing process follows the format in *The Path* by Laurie Beth Jones; it includes my variations and explanations.

Step 1) Ask, "God, what is your purpose for me?"

Your purpose is already there, inside you. So it's a matter of having a coach come alongside you and ask questions that draw out the beautiful aspects of how God created you.

Have you ever asked the question, "What on earth am I here for?"? According to Pastor and author Rick Warren, it is the most important question you will ever ask.

I'm betting you have asked that question, maybe many times. If you're like me, you've asked, "What on earth am I here for?" with a frown of frustration on your face, arms in the air and angst in your soul.

Let's modify our approach to the question.

We can ask our Creator, "God, what is your purpose for me?" Then there's awe, wonder, curiosity and calm in the asking. The asking becomes a heart-felt prayer. It's a question you may be prompted to ask repeatedly during this purpose journey.

Step 2) Identify Your "Serving" Verbs

"Each of you has been blessed with one of God's many wonderful gifts to be used in the service of others. Use your gift well."

1 Peter 4:10 CEV

Since your mission is about serving that means it requires action. You will *do something* with your gift. Look at the following verbs, action words: accomplish, build, connect, create, encourage, facilitate, heal, influence, inform, lead, move, plant, protect, provide, transform.

Which ones excite you? Of course, there are thousands of verbs available to us. What other verbs come to your mind when you think of serving? It's also fun to use a thesaurus for more ideas. Choose two or three verbs that appeal to you.

Step 3) Identify Your Gifts

"God has given each of us the ability to do certain things well."

Romans 12:6 NLT

What are your gifts? What do you do really well?

You may be able to answer that question quickly. However, I've found that most people *cannot* easily identify what they do well, quite possibly for two reasons.

1. The things we do well are so natural that we tend to think everyone can do them. So, we may not even recognize the gifts we have.

2. Even if we *are* able to recognize our gifts, it may be hard to say them out loud because it feels like bragging. If you're like me, you learned early on that you just do not "toot your own horn!" If that's the case for you, then I have a suggestion for a different way to think about it:

The things we do well are gifts from God. That mindset allows us to acknowledge the way he created us. We can even turn it into a prayer of thanks. For example, I can say, "Thank you, God, for making me enthusiastic, friendly, and encouraging."

What supernatural abilities has God given you that you can thank him for?

One more way to identify your gifts is to think of what other people say they appreciate about you. What do your parents, grandparents, friends, teachers and co-workers say they appreciate about you? You may even want to ask people you love and trust what they think your gifts are.

You are given the ability to do *certain* things well, not *all* things.

What a relief!

Step 4) Identify Your Passions

"If you can't figure out your purpose, figure out your passion. For your passion will lead you right into your purpose.
Stay patient and trust the journey."

-Bishop T.D. Jakes

What do you love to do? What dream is on your heart? What desire do you yearn for?

Identifying your passions helps you identify your purpose. It also can add joy, lots of joy, to your life. Robert Vallerand, a pioneer in the field of passion research, claims that participating in your passion can add eight hours of joy to your week. I invite you to participate in your passions and see how much joy you can add to your week.

You were wired with passions – intense emotions that drive you, strong feelings that stir your soul and convictions that compel you to take action. Let me tell you about Jennifer and Craig and passions that have compelled and propelled them.

Jennifer, my stepdaughter, is one of the most authentic people I know. As a little girl she played Spotlight for hours. With her pretend microphone and in the spotlight from an upturned lamp, she would perform Diana Ross songs. She followed her passion in high school and college, performing and studying opera. She is now teaching voice at the university level.

When people ask how she chose that career, Jennifer says, "I didn't. Music chose me."

That's how it is with a passion. It is so compelling it's like a magnet pulling you toward it. Your passion chooses you.

Craig has been passionate about the idea of owning his own business since he was in sixth grade. He was inspired by his friend's parents who owned a dry-cleaning business. He saw that they made their own decisions, and they worked hard. That clicked with him.

When he was in high school Craig's physics teacher recognized his outstanding math and science skills and encouraged Craig to consider engineering. In college he worked on a chemical engineering degree. He also took business classes and a course to learn business plan writing.

For over three decades, Craig has been a successful business owner; he brings out the best in people and generously contributes to the community. He loves being his own boss, and he loves developing and leading a team to make Team 1 Plastics successful for all stakeholders. Craig's passion to own his own business has been his North Star.

Think about your childhood. What did you love to do? What did you play? Those are clues to passions that may have been trying to choose you. Your passions are clues to your purpose.

Step 5)   Identify a Need in the World that Tugs at Your Heart

What need in the world causes you to cry? What need in the world makes you angry? What message do you want to shout from the rooftops?

> **"Your purpose/God's plan for your life lies at the intersection of your passion and a need in the world."**

That quote has stuck in my mind for years. (I would give credit where credit is due if I could find who said it.)

Here is the application of the quote about purpose in my life:

My passion is teaching, reading and sharing all the wonderful things I learn. And socializing!

A need in the world that tugs at my heart is joy – the world needs more joy! If people have more joy, they'd have more energy, more focus and more strength. With more joy in each person, more people would be served – encouraged, fed, educated, revived, healed and fulfilled! If people have more joy, there would be less stress and worry, less wasted time and money. With joy, life is just plain more fun.

Step 6)   Identify Your Core Values

What do you want people to say about you at your 90th birthday party? What legacy do you want to leave? What do you stand for? What values guide your decisions and actions? Answers to those questions are clues to your core values.

Some core values of people I've coached are compassion, freedom, faith, authenticity and hope. This is about identifying what is already inside you. While it may be helpful to look at lists of personal core values, it will be more helpful to think about the values that guide your decisions and actions.

Step 7) Write Your Rough Drafts

I recommend taking a week or even two weeks to ponder and complete the first six steps. Then you are ready to write your rough draft. This is another really fun part. Got your smile on, your favorite music, and/or a friend by your side?

I say *rough drafts* because you'll be writing many different sentences that could capture the essence of who you are. It's not about perfection. Write whatever comes to your mind, no censoring. You may want to use a thesaurus. It's fine to have a page or more of rough drafts; it gives us more to work with as we wordsmith your mission statement. Approach it playfully!

You may use either mission-statement format:

My mission is to: _____   _____
                          (your verb)   (your core value)

God put me on
this earth to: _____   _____
                          (your verb)   (your core value)

This part of the coaching process is so fun! We play with the ideas and the words until the essence of you appears in your mission statement – and we word it in a way that really excites you.

Then you can post it everywhere – on your mirror where you see it first thing in the morning and on your bedside table where you see it before you fall asleep every night. You could post it on the dashboard of your vehicle. Maybe you'll even make it your screensaver. It will become imprinted on your heart. When people ask you what you do, you won't tell them your job – you will proclaim your purpose!

Points to Ponder

1. What are your gems from the Discover Your Purpose chapter?

2. What are your passions?

3. What are your core values?

4. What will you do to discover your mission statement?

Part Two

Spark Joy ~
Mind, Body and Spirit

Jan Glowe-Janke

Chapter 3

Stay C. A. L. M.

"Calm is a superpower."

-Brené Brown

"Stay CALM; don't panic!" our guide told us.

Let's go back to the banks of the beautiful Bow River. In the introduction I told you about our warm, sunny July day in the Canadian Rockies. We were outfitted in wetsuits, life-jackets and helmets. Just before we put our inflatable rafts into the river for our white-water rafting adventure, our guide gathered the group and gave us instructions, again. He reminded us, "Always listen to your guide!"

He continued, "If you get thrown out of the boat, just cross your arms over your chest, put your feet out in front of you and let the river carry you until another raft can rescue you. Stay CALM; don't panic!"

I thought, "Stay CALM. It sounds good, and it makes perfect sense. When I'm calm, my head is clear. I can think better, feel better and act in healthy, helpful ways.

But just *how* do I stay calm when I hit rough waters? *How* do I stay calm if I get thrown out of the boat?"

You have probably asked questions like that too:

How do I stay calm in the midst of pain and uncertainty?

How do I stay calm in the midst of constant criticism and negativity?

How do I stay calm when it feels like everything is falling apart?

Calm in the COVID Crisis

"Stay CALM" is the "message" I was getting in mid-March, 2020, as the coronavirus ran rampant, claimed lives and put fear in the hearts of people all over the world.

We were told, "Stay home. If you must go out, keep your distance; stay at least six feet from others. Wear masks to cover your nose and mouth. Wear gloves. Wash your hands."

Schools closed. Churches closed. Restaurants shut their doors. Sporting events were cancelled. Businesses shut down. Unemployment reached unprecedented heights. Life as we knew it came to a screeching halt. Fear and uncertainty gripped our hearts.

God was persistent in his message to me: "Stay CALM, Jan, and help others stay CALM."

Here is my SPLASH of C.A.L.M. for you, my friend, a word for each letter to help you get beyond crumbling, step up above simply surviving so you can radiantly thrive – for your good and for the good of all.

It's a message to remember, and it can help you STAY CALM in any situation.

C – Control

"… we take captive every thought to make it obedient to Christ."

2 Corinthians 10:5 NIV

Focus on the things you CAN control.

There is one thing we can control, and it has the power to change everything. Every. Single. Thing. We can control which thoughts to focus on.

Accept those things you cannot control. Don't complain. Don't whine. Move past those things you cannot control. We cannot control the coronavirus. We can't control all the events that are cancelled. We may not like it, but for our sanity, we must accept it.

We can think of all the things that are *not* cancelled – and be grateful. Being outdoors is not cancelled. Laughing is not cancelled. Talking is not cancelled. We can still go for walks and bike rides. We can still sing and dance. We can talk on the phone. We can Face Time with our friends and family, and we can gather on Zoom.

Many people are choosing to think of the forced slow-down as a blessing; they see opportunity in this "Forced Sabbatical." They are using this extra time to spend with family, to get healthier, to work on a project, or to learn something new.

Laura is learning to play bagpipes. Kim has ordered an afghan kit; she'll learn to crochet. Jonathan wants to watch *Star Wars* in Spanish so he can learn a language. Tom bought a mountain bike, and his goal is to ride 2,000 miles by the end of the year. Linda is sorting through old family pictures and delving into her ancestry.

Many people are blessing others by offering their services for free. Sam Horn, the Intrigue Expert, world-renowned author and keynote speaker, started a Facebook group, "So You Want to Write a Book." Every day starting mid-March, 2020, she showed up at noon and so did I, excitedly! Truly, she was an answer to prayer. Sam provided the nudge and knowledge I needed to write and finish this book for you.

It is essential for us to *control the thoughts we focus on*. When we accept those things we cannot control, maintain our faith and gratitude, we can move forward. We can learn and grow and be adaptable.

A – Adaptability

"Adaptability is being able to adjust to any given set of circumstances at any given time."
-Coach John Wooden

When it comes to adaptability, we have three choices. [7] We can:

1. Crumble

2. Simply survive

3. Radiantly thrive

Here's a brief description of each stage of adaptability:

1. Crumble – fall apart, feel frozen with fear; paralyzed, can hardly breathe

2. Simply survive – just get by; no prosperity, no joy

3. Radiantly thrive – purpose-driven, empowered by faith and gratitude; everybody benefits

You can *radiantly thrive* . . . one smile, one kind word, one grateful thought, one hope-full prayer, one playful moment, one purposeful step forward at a time.

> *"Surviving is important. Thriving is elegant."*
> -Maya Angelou

🐾🐾🐾🐾🐾🐾🐾

In 2015 Jeff Boss wrote, "The need for adaptability has never been greater than it is now." Five years later, with the coronavirus pandemic, the need for adaptability has become tremendously essential! Mr. Boss' article, "14 Signs of an Adaptable Person" identifies specific characteristics to incorporate into our own thinking and being. [8] I'll share seven signs. As you read, you might consider which ones you do well, and choose one you want to improve.

An adaptable person:

1. "Has the will – the emotional tolerance, mental fortitude, spiritual guidance – to not only face uncertainty but smack it in the face and press on."

2. Is able to grow and change

3. Sees opportunities

4. Doesn't whine (if they can't control it, they move on)

5. Is open-minded (is curious, keeps learning)

6. Engages in positive self-talk

7. "Knows what they stand for. Choosing to adapt to something new, forego the old, requires a strong understanding of personal values."

One thing we know for sure: In this world we will have troubles and struggles. Being able to adjust to any situation, being adaptable, allows us to be of good cheer when we're forced to take detours on the road to our desired destinations.

Controlling the thoughts we focus on and being adaptable are powerful strategies that equip us to step beyond simply surviving into radiant thriving.

L – Limit the News

When it comes to watching the news, I am tempted to be like an ostrich and bury my head in the sand, mainly for two reasons: The news is often disturbing, and I'm not sure who to trust to deliver the news. At the other extreme of head-in-the-sand are those who watch the news constantly.

Being informed is important. Being wise and deliberate about our news consumption is even more important. How can we be informed without getting overwhelmed?

Strategies for an Intentional Approach to News Consumption

1. Take control. Make a conscious decision about how much time and what time of day works best for you to consume the news. Turn off news notifications on your smartphone.
2. Be savvy. Evaluate news sources for bias and accuracy. A website such as
   https://mediabiasfactcheck.com/
   offers evaluations of many worldwide news sources. That information can help you avoid disturbing, inaccurate reporting.
3. Focus. Spend your time on the issues you find most important.
4. Reflect. Be mindful of the impact that news is having on your sense of well-being. Make adjustments accordingly. For example, I cannot watch news first thing in the morning, and I absolutely cannot watch it before bed and expect to sleep. Each of us needs to find a time of day that works best.

To stay CALM, let's limit the news. We can be informed and still have time, energy and a joyful spirit to act on many activities that truly matter to us.

M – Meditate

One expert said, "Meditation is like brushing our teeth. It's a cleansing process that allows us better health. We do it, brushing our teeth and meditating, not so much for the enjoyment of the experience, but for the benefits it brings to our every-day lives."

If you're hesitant about meditating, some of Dr. Paul Dugliss' teachings might ease your mind. He says meditation is all about letting go. It clears the nervous system. If you're like me and you have a busy mind, too many thoughts, no problem. Dr. Dugliss says that's actually part of the clearing process. You may even fall asleep. Whatever happens in meditation, we just accept it without judging it.

http://www.HeartBasedMeditation.com

🐾🐾🐾🐾🐾🐾🐾

Julie Matteson Warfield is one of the most loving people I know. Accepting. Inclusive. Compassionate. I marvel at her beautiful, calm Spirit and her ability to be fully present. A walk with Julie is to notice and appreciate the majesty and unique characteristics of a tree, or 20 trees, the wonder of a praying mantis, and the intricacy of a sunflower on the path. Being with Julie soothes my Spirit and smooths out the wrinkles in my soul. She is beyond-this-world wise, and humble. Julie needed to be persuaded to share that she has a master's degree in Divinity. She knows turbulent waters and severe storms, yet she is a picture of "elegant thriving."

Julie's purpose is to usher in the pure, loving presence of God. She does that with a daily meditation practice, with every word she speaks and with every prayer she prays. May you feel his love and Julie's as you read the following mediation message she wrote for you.

"Meditation is a tried and true path to returning to our true selves. Meditation is an inner journey to balancing our human be-ing with our human do-ing. Our body/minds are continually seeking balance. Spending time in meditation invites us to acknowledge the internal balancing intelligence within each of us.

The mind is an incredible tool. But humans, in our proclivity to edge God out, have identified with the mind so completely, we believe it is who we are. *It is not.*

We are not the noisy chattering voice in our head that is constantly bringing us anxiety and fear. *We are not our thoughts.*

We observe the thoughts that arise, allowing them to just be. We place no judgement or label upon them. In the Presence of God, we simply observe the mind and allow the thoughts to float away as clouds drift across the sky. We are the vast sky; our thoughts are simply passing clouds.

When we meditate, we get out of our own way, and allow the body/mind to return to its state of dynamic restfulness, inner peace and quiet. As the mind is hushed with the use of a mantra, feeling the power of the Holy Spirit coursing within each of our living cells or by simply placing our alert attention on the breath, an opening to the presence of God arises. Here we experience who we are. Here we are healed and brought home."

Jeanette – A Picture of CALM in the Storm

I'm happy to introduce you to Jeanette. She is crystal clear about her purpose, and she is choosing to *radiantly thrive* in the midst of this coronavirus storm. She had a yoga studio and taught classes in three locations – *before* the Stay Home order.

In my "What on Earth Am I Here For?" Workshop, we discovered her God-given purpose. *God put Jeanette on this earth to empower others to thrive.*

In the crunch of the coronavirus, I received an email from Jeanette, an invitation to her new *online* yoga studio! She had been making videos, making adjustments – adapting. When life and work as we know it changed drastically, Jeanette chose to focus on what she could control.

She writes, "Thank you for the gift of my mission statement. It has been a powerful tool in helping me *quickly regain my focus* when I found myself unemployed. *Instead of panicking or self-pitying* I was able to come back to my purpose. I could assess the gifts and talents God has given me and figure out how I can use my gifts to empower others to thrive. *I cannot fix COVID-19, but I can help others* maintain healthy bodies and minds through yoga and mindfulness."

(You can find Jeanette on her Facebook page, *BeFITting Body/Mind Connections*.)

Just like Jeanette, you can stay CALM in any situation. Remember to focus on things you can control, be adaptable, limit the news and meditate.

Points to Ponder

1. What are your gems from the Stay Calm chapter?

2. Which quality of CALM do you do well?

    Celebrate that!

3. Choose one quality of CALM you want to improve. What will you do to improve?

Jan Glowe-Janke

Chapter 4

Relax

"We will be more successful in all our endeavors if we can let go of the habit of running all the time, and take little pauses to relax and re-center ourselves, and we'll also have a lot more joy in living."
- Thich Nhat Hanh

The next three chapters are Relax, Refresh and Renew. For the purpose of discussion, we will have a specific focus for each chapter. In this relax chapter we will focus on the body. In Refresh we will focus on the Spirit, and in Renew we'll focus on the mind. The body, mind and spirit are intertwined, so connected that whatever good we do for one area will splash into and positively affect all areas.

Relax Your Body

Do you crave quiet and CALM? Do you yearn for moments of peace, a place where you can sit back, breathe and be yourself? Would you love to have a sanctuary, a place to step away from struggles and soothe your soul?

It is possible. Not only can you go to that sanctuary anytime, anywhere, you can visit your sanctuary for one minute, seven minutes, or an hour a day.

Calming your body is not only possible, it is essential. Take time for stillness so you can be the best, most joyful version of yourself.

Relax. It's a verb, an action word. That seems ironic because relaxing can mean resting and doing nothing. Doing nothing is an action! I tend to get hung up thinking that I have to be doing something – productive.

> *"Sometimes the most productive thing*
> *you can do is relax."*
>
> -Mark Black

When we relax, we are doing something very productive for our health. Relaxation slows heart rate and breathing rate, lowers blood pressure, improves digestion, helps maintain normal blood sugar levels, reduces the activity of stress hormones, reduces muscle tension and chronic pain, improves concentration and mood, improves sleep quality, lowers fatigue, reduces anger and frustration, and relaxation boosts confidence to handle problems. [9]

Relaxing the body has a lovely ripple effect. The benefits to our physical health ripple into our mental and emotional well-being.

What are your favorite ways to relax? You may listen to soothing music, soak in a warm bath, meditate, write or create art. Maybe you enjoy yoga, deep breathing or massage. Wherever you relax, that is your sanctuary.

Intentional Daily Downtime

> *"Almost everything will work again*
> *after you unplug it. Including you."*
>
> -Anne Lamott

Relaxation requires unplugging. Yes, that means leaving your phone behind. Leave it in another room so you don't hear it and you're not tempted to look at it. Really UNPLUG so you can ease into stillness. Besides your phone, what else do you need to unplug from – iPad, people, expectations, your to-do list, work, worries, or responsibilities?

Once you unplug, then what? I'll give you three ideas for your daily downtime, then we'll talk about sleep, your nighttime sanctuary.

1) *Sit Spot*

> *"Rest is not idleness, and to lie sometimes on the grass*
> *under trees on a summer's day, listening to the*
> *murmur of the water, or watching the clouds float*
> *across the sky, is by no means a waste of time."*
>
> - John Lubbock

"What do you do to relax?" I asked Sheri. She told me two ideas that I can hardly wait to share with you. First she replied, "I go to my Sit Spot."

I was intrigued. "Your what?" I asked.

"Everyone can benefit from having a Sit Spot," she explained. "It's a special place nearby in nature, close enough you can visit daily. It can be a front step, backyard, nearby park or lake. There is no right or wrong location. Allow your inner pull to guide you. It's a place where you feel grounded and close to nature." [10]

Your Sit Spot feels like a sanctuary to you. Mary's Sit Spot is her screened-in porch. She enjoys being in fresh air as she admires the pond, woods and the sky. There is awe and appreciation in her voice as she talks about all the shades of green, the flowers and flurry of birds.

Becky's Sit Spot is her canopied, cushioned bench swing that coworkers gave her as a retirement gift. She looks out over the yard, tiki bar and lake. She says, "As soon as I sit, my mind settles, and I feel the aaaahhh seep into my soul."

Alex, my friend and former student, loves the outdoors. He wrote, "I close my eyes and listen to all the sounds. And I smell the wind to decipher the scents. Hearing and smelling are the least used senses we have."

When weather doesn't allow you to be outside, simply find a Sit Spot where you can enjoy the outdoors and nature through a window.

What are possible Sit Spots for you? Make a habit of treating yourself to time in your Sit Spot.

2) *Rest Hour*

> *"You have enough. You do enough.*
> *You are enough. RELAX."*
>
> -Author unknown

After Sheri told me about her Sit Spot, she described the daily Rest Hour at church camp. It was right after lunch, for everyone. Sheri had attended camp for many years as a caring adult to encourage her group of middle school students and to be a support to staff. This particular year Rest Hour had a greater impact on her than ever before.

Sheri said, "Napping, reading or visiting quietly with a cabin mate were acceptable options, but on many days that week a nap happened. I was amazed at how much better my day went with this refreshing boost each afternoon. It made sense after an early rise to my day. The nap gave me the energy to be my best self – mind, body and spirit – through the afternoon and evening.

"I cherished intentional daily downtime. I craved it, and I brought the concept home with me. However, good intentions can be easier said than done, especially when I was back into life's normal routine. I found it difficult to honor that time. Even after blocking it out on my calendar, I allowed phone calls or Zoom meetings to carry into my Rest Hour.

"Finally, I realized I was not prioritizing this time for me. If I was going to reap the benefits, I had to honor that time. Now, I will be flexible as life requires, by moving it up or back slightly, I schedule appointments around it and let people know I am not available during that time. I have a special appointment scheduled – me!"

If a rest hour, or even part of an hour, sounds like a sanctuary to you, consider scheduling – and honoring – your own daily rest hour.

3) *Breath*

> *"Feelings come and go like clouds in a windy sky.*
> *Conscious breathing is my anchor."*
>
> -Thich Nhat Hanh

You can step into your own private sanctuary with focus on your breath.

When we are stressed or nervous, our breath becomes shallow. We might hunch our shoulders, clench our teeth or tighten muscles without realizing it.

Most of us must learn how to breathe deeply. Sue, my friend and yoga teacher, showed us how to breathe like a baby. (You can actually see a baby's belly expand as she inhales.) Sue instructed us, "Put your hand on your belly, just below your waist. When you inhale deeply the air goes into your belly and your hand rises." It took a lot of practice for me to learn to breathe deeply; now I love it.

Let tension in your shoulders or a knot in your stomach be a trigger to remind you to take slow, deep breaths. When you feel anxious, pay attention to how it affects your body. Taking your attention to the spot that is tense will take your breath there, and that tense spot will be soothed.

🌢🌢🌢🌢🌢🌢🌢

Here are three breathing practices to help you relax. Experiment with them to find which ones are a fit for you.

1) Yahweh

As you inhale, think "Yah;" as you exhale, think "weh." Yahweh is the exclusive and sacred name for God used by the ancient Hebrews.

2) Inhale God's love; exhale your love to him.

When I tried this breathing practice suggested by modern-day mystic and podcaster, James Finley, an interesting thing happened. A beautiful thing, really.

As I inhaled, I began to hear God's whisper in my heart, "I love you, Janet."

Then I exhaled my love for him along with my silent words, "I love you, God." With every breath, a smile happened naturally. This breathing practice is a lovely way to relax into God's love. I hope you try it and that it soothes your soul too.

3) "I easily relax, let go and trust you, God."

That is my go-to mantra for calming breath, especially at night if I'm having difficulty falling asleep. On the inhale, think, "I easily relax." On the long, slow exhale, think, "I easily let go and trust you, God." Repeat. Relax.

Sleep, Your Nighttime Downtime

Karolyn's sons were seven and two years old. When I asked her what she wanted for her birthday, she immediately replied, "A nap!"

If you are sleep-deprived like Karolyn, "perhaps the single most spiritual thing you could do right now is to put this book down and take a nap." I laughed out loud when I read that in John Ortberg's book, *The Life You've Always Wanted*. It's true – sleep is essential!

What happens if you don't get the sleep you need?

I'll admit that I get grumpy and groggy when I lack sleep. My mom used to say, "Take a hot bath and things will look better in the morning." Isn't that the truth? When you're rested, everything looks better and brighter.

Turns out, I'm normal when it comes to symptoms of not enough sleep—grumpy and groggy, and the experts agree with my mom.

"First and foremost, we need to make sleep a priority," writes Dr. Harneet Walia, sleep expert at the Cleveland Clinic. Most adults need seven to nine hours of sleep a night. Sleep deprivation is dangerous, and it has a negative impact on your health. Too little sleep causes short-term problems such as lack of alertness, excessive daytime sleepiness and relationship stress. Lack of sleep even increases the likelihood of car accidents. Chronic sleep deprivation can lead to more long-term and serious health problems like high blood pressure, diabetes, heart attack and stroke. More potential problems associated with sleep deprivation are obesity, depression, lower sex drive and weakened immune system. It also causes premature wrinkles and dark circles under the eyes. [11]

If your body is telling you to sleep better and longer, consider this advice from Cleveland Clinic's Dr. Michelle Drerup: 1) Schedule adequate time for sleep. 2) Keep a consistent wake-up time, and 3) Relax before bed. She suggests soaking in a warm bath or reading a book to relax. Dr. Drerup also recommends putting away the smart phone or tablets at least an hour before bedtime.
4) Unplug. Then your bedroom becomes your nighttime sanctuary.

I can almost hear you thinking, "But I can never get everything done so I could go to bed by ten o'clock." Or "I cannot afford the luxury of sleeping eight hours." Or "I don't have time to take a nap." Please take this seriously: You are essential, and sleep is essential for your good health. When you understand the utmost importance of sleep, you are empowered to make it a priority.

"Sleep is an act of trust: I am reminded when I go to sleep that the world is in God's hands, not mine."
-John Ortberg

We'll end this chapter with an evening prayer that you may want to print, put by your bed and pray every night.

Jan Glowe-Janke

An Evening Prayer

Lord,
It is night.
The night is for stillness.
Let me be still in the presence of God.

It is night after a long day.
What has been done has been done;
what has not been done has not been done;
let it be.

The night is dark.
Let my fears of the darkness of the world and of my own life
rest in you.

The night is quiet.
Let the quietness of your peace enfold me,
all dear to me,
and all who have no peace.

The night heralds the dawn.
Let me look expectantly to a new day,
new joys,
new possibilities.
In your name I pray.
Amen
(source unknown)

Points to Ponder

1. What are your gems from the Relax chapter?

2. What is one idea about relaxation you will put into action?

3. What is one thing you will do to improve your sleep habit?

Jan Glowe-Janke

Chapter 5

Refresh

"A good laugh and a long sleep are the two best cures for anything."

-Irish proverb

What Refreshes You?

I asked my Facebook friends that question. Their delightful answers refresh me! The top fifteen most popular responses were about friends and family (especially grandkids), nature, water, laughter, music, activity, reading, gratitude, prayer, pets, camping, art, gardening and projects.

Here's an unusual response that I must share with you. Rebecca said, "Crying refreshes me." Certainly not your typical answer, but crying definitely can be cleansing, and it can restore your strength.

"The cure for anything is salt water. Sweat, tears or the sea."

-Isak Dinesen

There's a wonderful variety of ways to revive your Spirit. Get your "refreshment radar" working, and be continually on the lookout for whatever might cheer you.

Trifecta of Refreshment

1) *Move*

Coach Vranda was our friend, a modern-day saint who refreshed others in a multitude of ways. She'd show up at track meets with food for all the kids on the team, she served at our local Make a Difference House, and she continually poured loving attention into her many friends and family members. Vranda is especially famous for her one-word mantra.

It's a mantra that will live forever in the hearts and minds of every athlete she ever coached – and anyone within earshot. She didn't just say it, didn't even just yell it . . . She trumpeted it! That bellowing command sounded like, "MOOOOVE!" And we would be wise to follow her command.

Our bodies are designed to move. You've probably heard that "sitting is the new smoking." When we are sedentary, we open the door to all kinds of health problems. Movement is vital for a healthy lymphatic system, and the lymphatic system is vital for our immunity. It does not have a pump of its own like the circulatory and respiratory systems. Our movement is the pump that stimulates the lymphatic system which keeps us robust in fighting toxins and diseases.

Movement is a lifestyle for people who live in the Blue Zones. For longer, healthier life we can copy their genius. Moderate, physical activity like walking and gardening is a natural part of their daily lives. Movement is a great way to get refreshed, even if -- especially if -- we don't feel like it. And movement with a friend enhances the health benefits.

2) *Socially Connect*

When I was in my teen years, Dad often asked me, "Do you ever do anything by yourself?" Instinctively, I've always known that every activity is more fun with a friend. I often reminded him I learned from his example. Dad was a very social guy; he loved being active and engaged with his family and his friends. Do you crave social connections too?

If you are one who thoroughly enjoys time with people, I don't need to convince you that being socially connected makes you healthier and happier. If you are *not* naturally outgoing, it's important to know that social connections are vital to your health and longevity. Research shows that social isolation is just as much a threat to longevity as smoking or obesity. That's just one good reason to make an effort to spend more time in social activities.

Consider finding a club involving your favorite hobby or scheduling a game night with friends. What will you do to be connected to people?

Consider volunteering. It's one more way to connect socially. It's one of the Blue Zones' secrets that can add four to fourteen healthy, happy years to your life.

Volunteering is a beautiful thing. As we give of ourselves, our love and time and energy, it fills a need in the world. At the same time, it fills a need in us.

That's how it was for Sheila. After she retired, she was meeting friends for lunches. She enjoyed time with friends, but it just wasn't enough. She felt like something was missing. Sheila invited me to coach her.

We discovered and wrote her mission statement. *God put Sheila on this earth to create an environment where others can feel loved and treasured.* She had created that loving environment with her own daughters as they were growing up and with her students. In retirement, she felt the void that comes with not serving.

In coaching sessions, we explored how Sheila might fill that void. She decided to call a local women's center. She met with the director and began to volunteer there. Sheila especially enjoys meeting with clients, supporting them, loving on them, praying for them (with their permission). She said, "You can just see the appreciation in their faces."

Volunteering is refreshing to those who are served and to the one who is serving.

If you're thinking, "But I'm not retired" – no problem. You could consider sharing your professional expertise with others. Maybe there's a co-worker or someone on your career path to regularly encourage. Perhaps you could mentor someone or start a study group. Ways to serve are endless.

Maybe you've been thinking you'd like to volunteer, and maybe you already know who or what group you'd like to serve. Great! Here's a nudge for you. Make the call. Offer your idea and see where it leads. Don't be concerned that it might not work; you can keep searching till you find a good fit.

Right after I retired from education, I tried volunteering as a worker in the office in our church. Notice I said, "Tried?" It didn't take long to know that was not a good fit. Being in a dark office, by myself, was absolutely not where I wanted to be. I shifted gears.

I thought about my passions. I love reading, talking about books, and I was really missing reading to my students. So, I called some assisted living homes. One home nearby was open to having me come in for an hour a week to read to senior citizens. The best part of reading to folks was the hello-hugs all around, the personal stories and laughter generated by the reading, and good-bye, see-you-next-week hugs. It was a good fit, for many years.

What are your passions? How could you put your passions to work in your community?

If you are feeling the Nudge to volunteer, just look for opportunities in your community. Think about ways you could put your talents to work. Talk to someone about your idea. You could call a local church, food pantry, women's shelter, assisted-living home, hospital, school, museum, park, or community center. Some communities have actual volunteer organizations.

When we focus on helping others we put our own worries and anxieties at rest.

Kathy's God-given purpose, her mission, is to nourish others. She nourishes others with attentive listening and encouraging words, written and spoken. She sends beautiful cards with sweet, loving messages. On the front of a card she recently sent me was this message, "You are a downright glorious spectacle of a human being!" How refreshing!

Kathy said, "As I nourish others, I get nourished."

She seemed surprised by that. She even admitted feeling a little guilty. But that's the way God designed it! *"Those who refresh others will themselves be refreshed"* *(Proverbs 11:25).*

You've experienced that too, haven't you? Maybe you visited someone in the hospital. Or you called a friend who was going through rough waters. You did it from your compassionate heart. Your presence, your kindness, your prayers blessed others. But afterwards, you probably felt like you were the one most blessed.

3) *Spend Time in Nature*

"I go to nature to be soothed and healed, and to have my senses put in tune once more."
                                        -John Burroughs

Where is your most relaxing, calming place in nature? Maybe you're most at home in the mountains. Or perhaps you find peace in the woods. Or do you feel like you're home when you are on or near the water? For me, water provides a sanctuary. A beach is my best, most relaxing place to be, my slice of heaven. I love warm sun on my face, the feel of salty air and my toes in soft sand.

As you step into nature, physically and/or mentally, step away from your responsibilities, worries, and thoughts of doing. Joyce Meyer often reminds us, "We are human be-ings, not human do-ings." Write yourself a permission slip to take a break from being productive. Be open to what you see, hear and feel. Be aware, be accepting and be grateful.

Whatever your sanctuary is, treat yourself to it. Go there physically as often as possible. When you can't be there physically, place yourself mentally in the peace of your sanctuary. Let it soothe your soul.

❧ ❧ ❧ ❧ ❧ ❧ ❧

Can you name the saint who found God in everything in nature? If you're a Catholic "kid," you probably know immediately. Yes, we're talking about Saint Francis of Assisi, the 12th century mystic. He saw God in trees, worms and lonely flowers by the side of the road.

Marcie, Lindy and my dad delight in nature. Marcie, like Saint Francis, sees God in flowers. She writes, "Being quarantined and unable to be with friends and family, the days seem long, and we long for this to be over. On my walk in March, I came across a hyacinth that was just beginning to bloom. That very small flower in someone's very brown yard brought me joy. It was a sign of hope and new beginnings. That refreshed my spirit and brightened my day."

Lindy enjoys watching a bluebird investigate the bluebird house in her yard. Sue loves seeing porcupines on their property and pileated woodpeckers in their neighborhood. Mary is delighted by the arrival of wood ducks on her pond.

My dad seemed to notice and appreciate everything in nature from sunsets to all kinds of critters. He had a gift for spotting pheasants as much as a mile away, or so it seemed. To this day, when I see a pheasant, I feel Dad's joy blend with my own.

🐾🐾🐾🐾🐾🐾🐾

In the trifecta of refreshment – movement, social connections, immersing yourself in nature – what are your most refreshing things to do? Once you identify ideas for your own refreshment, will you schedule one into your week? Or better yet, treat yourself to at least a few minutes each day to revive your Spirit.

Points to Ponder

1. What are your gems from the Refresh chapter?

2. What volunteer opportunities appeal to you?

3. What will you do to incorporate at least one refreshing activity into your week?

Chapter 6

Renew

"... Be transformed by the renewing of your mind."
Romans 12:2 NIV

Dad worked for a utility company. He always pointed out utility poles and electrical lines. Because of Dad I know that a transformer is the gray box toward the top of the pole where lines appear to connect. What really happens in that gray box is a transformation of energy. Very high (dangerous) voltage goes into the gray box where it is *transformed* into electrical current that is safe and useful to the consumer. Transformed.

Renewing our minds does the same transforming work as the gray box.

What does it mean to renew our minds? And how do we do that?

According to Merriam Webster, "Renew implies a *restoration* of what had become faded or disintegrated so it seems like new." And *restore* implies a return to an original state after a depletion or loss."

Restoring is exactly what Todd and Sue are doing to their forest and meadow.

They are in the process of restoring 15 acres of forest. They want to re-establish the wooded area and an adjacent meadow for wildlife. They called in a forestry professional for an assessment. He told them within five years, many of the mature trees would start to decay. They hired loggers who came in the wintertime when the ground was frozen so as not to damage the floor of the forest. They cut selectively, leaving the oak, birch and maple trees. Throughout the cut area, seedlings will sprout up naturally and abundantly. Todd and Sue reseeded areas so there will be a natural food plot to nourish animals.

To restore the meadow, they consulted with wildlife specialists. Beginning with the end in mind, the goal was to establish native grasses and wildflowers to support pollinators. They plowed and tilled the land, eliminated the woody brush and reseeded with fast-growing oats to kill the weeds. Late in the fall they will plant native flowers and grasses in preparation for the spring growing season.

There's great joy in a restoration project, in renewing something to its original beauty and purpose!

Just as Todd and Sue are restoring land, we can restore our minds. There's not only joy in the *project*, you will experience joy in the *process* of renewing your mind.

The Process of Restoration

1. Identify where you are currently. (That may mean asking for help.)

2. Identify where you want to be. (Begin with the end in mind.)

3. Identify the weeds/mindsets preventing growth, life and joy.

4. Transform or "choke out" the weeds/weedy mindsets.

5. Plant nourishing, life-giving seedlings/renewed mindsets.

Our natural state is love, joy and peace; a state of mind that gives life and beauty to us and others. Even as I write that, I realize you might not agree. I'm inviting you to stay with me, keep an open mind as you continue reading. Have faith. Maybe you'll learn, or be reminded, that thoughts are *the key*! Our thoughts tremendously impact on our words, actions and behavior.

> *"If you change the way you look at things,*
> *the things you look at change."*
> -Wayne Dyer

Here is really good news: We *can* change the way we look at things. We have the power to transform thoughts that are *not* in alignment with who we really are and who we are created to be. Let me remind you of the truth about you – you are God's masterpiece, you are one of a kind, and you are extraordinary! You were created for a purpose. It is essential to have – or grow – mindsets that empower you to live your God-given purpose.

While we can't choose the thoughts that "appear" in our minds, we can definitely decide to keep those that are serving us well. And we can choose to transform those thoughts that are dangerous or unhealthy.

Mindsets

Most often, renewing our minds means we have to let go of old ways of thinking. Our old, habitual ways of thinking are so deeply ingrained in our subconscious that we probably are unaware of them. My coaches have helped tremendously in deepening my awareness of old thinking habits. For example, when Frank was coaching me, I said something about "my little brain." There was a long pause, and he called me on it. My tendency to think (and feel), "I'm not as good as . . ., not as smart as . . . others" showed up in my words. And it was holding me back from being all God has intended for me. Frank calls those thoughts "life patterns." You may have heard them called "limiting beliefs" or "programming." We're calling them mindsets.

How refreshing to know we do not have to believe everything we think!

Many of our mindsets are habits. To show you what I mean, I'll tell you about my favorite clock. It died – but not my habit of looking at it!

We have had a clock on our living room wall for over twenty years. One day over a month ago, the clock stopped. We tried several different new batteries, but nothing would bring my clock back to life. So we took it off the wall. I really miss it.

Countless times every day, my eyes automatically look where the clock used to be. I'm always startled it isn't there. Every time I look and don't see that clock, I'm reminded of a habit that I didn't even realize I had – much like habitual patterns of thinking. (If you're not sure what I'm talking about, try moving your kitchen garbage bag!)

Let's play a game to shine some light on thinking habits we've learned.

Finish the following sentences:

An apple a day _____.

Don't run with _____.

Don't judge a book _____.

If it's worth doing, _____.

Whatever you start, _____.

Your responses were automatic, weren't they? Those are sayings and quite possibly mindsets you learned early on, mindsets that may or may not be serving you well at this point in your life.

Mindsets that Refresh and Renew

Mindsets about "Failure"

"Whatever you start, you finish." That was a lesson I learned well from my parents. Did you learn that lesson too? While it may be true for some things, it is *not* true for *all* things. Let me explain.

A year after I retired from education, I joined a network marketing company. I loved the people, the company's mission and the personal growth component. I really believed it was going to provide solid income in my retirement. Well, it didn't turn out that way. I kept thinking, "I can't quit. I am not a quitter."

Thankfully I have a wise, loving stepdaughter and honest friends who pointed out the truth to me. My passion is coaching. Spending so much time and energy working my network marketing business was preventing me from growing a coaching business. It took many sleepless nights, a few years and lots of tears before I was ready to transform my thinking. Finally, I chose to step away from network marketing so I could step into work that I felt called to do.

Did you notice my words? I chose to say, "I stepped away from . . ." instead of using the word "quit." I also say "the business venture was a failure" instead of "I am a failure." Our words are powerful in shaping our thoughts and renewing our mindsets.

The business venture was a failure. But was it really?

It depends on how I think about it. I did not earn the income I had anticipated. In that sense, I guess you could say the business venture was a failure. Yet, there's no way I can call it a failure because so many blessings came from it. It was absolutely *not* a failure when I focus on all that I learned, the fabulous speakers I heard in person and classic authors I "met" in their books and recordings.

It was *not* a failure when I consider all the opportunities to step out of my comfort zone and gain self-confidence, all the re-connections with friends with whom I'd lost touch and the fun I had at company gatherings.

It was definitely *not* a failure when I think about the many wonderful life-long, life-changing friends I made! My mind is renewed as I reflect on all the good things that came from my time with the company, and I am transformed. Come to think of it, *network* marketing was wildly successful for me – in a totally different way than I expected!

"Everything Is an Experiment"

Stepping away from network marketing and into my calling to coach has swung the door wide open to new adventures. In an out-of-the-blue (God-designed!) way, I learned about Professional Christian Coaching Institute (PCCI). I've learned life-changing mindsets from Kim Avery, author of *The Prayer Powered Entrepreneur,* and from Chris McCluskey, founder of the Professional Christian Coaching Institute.

In her Marketing Momentum class, Kim teaches that "Everything is an experiment."

And Chris says, "If it's worth doing, it's worth doing . . . poorly."

I was shocked when I first heard Chris say that. Then I laughed out loud when I realized he means start now. Learn and improve as you go. That's a very refreshing mindset for those of us who tend toward perfectionism.

Those fresh, new mindsets give me courage to try new things, learn from whatever happens and keep moving forward – without self-criticism or guilt.

My new mindset: It takes courage to quit one venture and faith to step into your calling!

Reframe

You may have heard the term "reframe." Both terms, renew and reframe, describe a transformation in thinking that is conducive to healthier emotions and behaviors.

Reframe Thoughts about Rejection and Divorce

Dee's Story

My friend Dee was a Quaker pastor, an author, speaker and teacher. This is her story in her own words of how she was transformed by the renewing of her mind:

"I was seventeen when I met a gorgeous hunk of a guy. He wore a leather jacket and Mennon aftershave. He didn't have a car or job, but he did have excuses for everything.

When I realized that he lied with almost every sentence he spoke, I said I didn't think we should see each other anymore. He told me we should get married and he threatened to kill himself if I refused.

I was a Christian girl who didn't know the answer to that – which is that he could kill himself if he decided to, but I wouldn't take the blame for his decision. I didn't know to say that. I believed he might do it, and it would be my fault so I married him and walked into hell for the next quarter of a century.

We had been married twenty-eight years when he told me that he needed his freedom. He said he felt we had married too young and he needed to find himself. He didn't mention that he would find himself with his best friend's wife.

I was devastated.

The father of my children might well be a villain and a rogue, but I had married him in church in front of God and witnesses, and I believed in the vows I made.

Desperate and feeling totally defeated, I talked to Elton Trueblood, a brilliant Quaker writer I had met at a conference I attended after I defied my husband and went to college.

Dr. Trueblood, a wise and kind man, recognized my pain. He smiled at me and said,

'My dear, he has freed you for better things.'

What a way to look at it! I wasn't being rejected, I was being freed.

Dr. Trueblood added, *'God will restore to you the years the locusts have eaten.'* (Joel 2: 25, 26) Those two sentences changed my life.

After I was freed from the bargain of that awful marriage, God filled my days with one adventure after another. He has restored to me the years the locusts had eaten."

Elton Trueblood's wise words helped Dee renew her mind. She was transformed from feeling rejected to feeling freed. Her devastation was transformed to hope. Her new mindsets allowed her to be resilient.

Reframe Thoughts about Death

My Grandpa's Death

When Grandpa died, I was in my early years of teaching, and Dad drove to my house to tell me. Dad wasn't a particularly religious man. Looking back though, I think he was probably spiritual in many ways, wise in God's ways. As he hugged me he said, "We lost our Grandpa today."

We reminisced about Grandpa; we cried and we laughed. Then there was a moment of heavy-hearted quiet. Dad said softly, "You know, God just loans people to us. They are not ours to keep." God loans people to us!

That mindset, the thought that each person is a gift from God, opened me up to deep gratitude. My thoughts shifted to thanking God for giving us our grandpa for so many years. And grateful thoughts let me feel moments of peace in the midst of grief.

Death by Suicide

It was a total shock, and it was beyond-words heart-wrenching. One of our sophomore students died by suicide. My counseling partner and I held an evening meeting for students, parents and staff. We invited a grief counselor to speak, and she brought a mom whose son had died by suicide when he was a senior in high school.

That dear mom talked about her shock at what some people said to her. One person told her, "Your son will never get into heaven."

She told us, "I believe that people who take their own lives are so broken that Jesus carries them into heaven." The picture she chooses to hold in her mind of Jesus carrying her son into heaven is a comfort to her. While nothing can take away the tragedy and the pain, the way we think can give us comfort and strength.

Reframe Thoughts about Depression

Parker Palmer's Story

Parker Palmer is a Quaker pastor and author who writes transparently about his struggles with depression. In one session his therapist pointed out Parker's current mindset and suggested a way that he might reframe it.

She said, "You seem to image what's happening to you as the hand of an enemy trying to crush you. Would it be possible to image it instead as the hand of a friend pressing you down to ground on which it's safe to stand?"

His first thought was that he needed a new (sane!) therapist and he felt insulted. He writes, "The image of depression as a befriending force began to work on me, slowly reframing my misery and helping me reclaim my mental health."

The reframe, the new way of thinking, allowed Pastor Palmer to begin to think of depression as a friend. That thought opened him to the valuable lessons that his friend depression could teach him. He was beginning to be transformed by the renewing of his mind. [12]

Renew Your Mindset about Sleep

Tim's Story

Tim's workday ended and the chills began – massive chills. He says, "I was shaking like I was in Alaska in the middle of winter without a coat." All night he was up every forty-five minutes. For two days straight, he did nothing. Then his leg started hurting. Throbbing. Every single day the pain worsened. Finally, at his wife's urging Tim went to the emergency room. They admitted him. He was forced to relax in the hospital for two days due to an infection.

Tim confessed that for most of his adult life he averaged four to five hours of sleep a night. He had a job, a wife and kids, and he took classes. He felt very responsible at his work. He also had a Sunday church job. In the back of Tim's mind was the example his father had set of workingTtwo jobs and sleeping very little. Tim thought, "This is what you do to support your family." Sleep was always low on his list of priorities.

Even before the pandemic, Tim began to feel tired of working all the time. When the pandemic hit and he could work from home, Tim began to transform his thinking. He let go of feeling so responsible and started prioritizing his health. He changed his mindset, and that led to changing some habits. He went to bed at ten and got up at six. He likes feeling less stressed, happier and more relaxed!

When I asked Tim the message he wanted to share with you, he said, "Don't let the responsibilities of life get in the way of things you need to do to have a life."

❧❧❧❧❧❧❧

To review and look forward, let's use two columns. You may want to look ahead at the juxtaposed lists so you have a visual. (The visual is available for download on https://janjanke.com). Sam Horn is the queen of juxtaposed lists; I learned this helpful technique from her.

The left column contains old habitual ways of thinking.

In the right column you'll see the transformed ways of thinking. These new mindsets keep us aligned with our purpose, our best selves.

Please consider making your own lists. As you become aware of a thought that appears automatically, write that thought on the left.

Reframe that old way of thinking; then write your renewed mindset in the column on the right.

OLD Mindset ⇨ **TRANSFORMED** ⇨ NEW Mindset

OLD Mindset	NEW Mindset
I'll have time to sleep on the weekend.	Sleep is essential for my health.
Quitting is not an option.	Quitting allows me to step into my calling.
What if I fail?	"Everything is an experiment."
I need to get this right/perfect.	"If it's worth doing— it's worth doing poorly."
What will others think?	What others think of me is none of my business.
I am stuck (in this job, town, marriage)	I choose to stay (in this job, town, marriage)
I don't know how.	I don't know how—yet!
What if this doesn't work out?	This—or something better!
I'm out of my comfort zone.	I'll do it scared anyway.
I should …	I choose to …
Everything is falling apart!	Everything is falling into place.

Points to Ponder

1. What are your gems from the Renew chapter?

2. What old, habitual ways of thinking do you want to transform?

3. What is your renewed or reframed way of thinking?

4. What benefits do you want to experience as a result of your renewed mindset?

Chapter 7

Create S. P. A. C. E.

*"Between stimulus and response there is a space
and in that space lies our power to choose."*
-Viktor Frankl

Nicky (not his real name) was a fourth grader in my class. All the other kids gave him a lot of room because they never knew when he might explode, and none of us ever knew what would trigger his explosions. He was a bright boy, but troubled. I knew things were rough at home, and I wanted school to be a safe place for him. I was baffled by Nicky's behavior and unsure about how to help him.

One day as the kids were leaving for the lunchroom and Nicky was calm, I caught him by himself. I said, "Nicky, I am really concerned about your outbursts of anger, for your sake and for your classmates. Could we talk about it and come up with some ideas?"

He agreed.

"Can you tell when you start to feel angry?" I asked.

He said, "Yes."

"Great! Then how might we stop you from letting anger get the best of you?"

As we talked it through, we thought a "time out" might help. At least it was worth a try.

We came up with a plan. When Nicky started to feel angry, he'd catch my attention and point to the door. He would leave the classroom, walk down the long hallway to the end and walk back. We notified the principal and other teachers about our plan. Our hope was that by the time he was back in the classroom, he would be cooled off, ready to cooperate and participate calmly.

Nicky just needed some SPACE.

Your S.P.A.C.E.

There are times when you and I feel frustrated or angry too, and we just want and need to get away. Think of a situation that causes you frustration or anxiety. What would happen if you chose to step away instead of getting tangled up in the emotion of the moment?

That step away is a step toward managing your emotions. You may actually leave the situation physically. Or you may mentally step away. Either way you have created a SPACE that permits you to *choose* your response. (Think RESPONSE-ability!)

When we create SPACE, we break out of old ways of thinking and feeling. We escape the trap of old habits that are not getting us the results we want. Here is a five-step method using the acronym of SPACE to help us create space to be our best selves.

Stop!

Pause (breathe)

Align with your mission statement (or love, joy, peace, whichever emotion you desire)

Choose your response

Evaluate your choice. Did it get the desired results?

Here's how that works:

When Nicky felt his temper rising, he <u>Stopped</u>.

His <u>Pause</u> was a walk down the hallway so he could

<u>Align</u> with his desire (and mine) to stay calm and in control of his emotions.

His <u>Choice</u> was to stay calm, rather than reacting (yelling, throwing a book or a chair).

<u>Evaluate</u> his choice. It worked! By stepping out of the classroom and taking a walk down the hall, he could prevent his temper getting the best of him, so the best of him could be enjoyed by all of us.

Land on Your Feet

We DO have the power to choose our response! Does that excite you as much as it does me?

Creating SPACE, following the five steps, flips us out of our old habits of reacting. We land on our feet, being our best selves! It starts with controlling our thoughts.

Think about a stressful situation where you can create SPACE. What's the stimulus that causes your blood pressure to rise, your frustration to flair? While you're thinking of a situation, I'll tell on myself.

I'm not too crazy about having to make dinner for Charlie and me every evening. But I do it. Sometimes without too much grumbling. So imagine my frustration when I have dinner on the table, I call him for dinner, and I get no answer. That's a stimulus for me, a recipe for resentment. He's usually in another room downstairs while I'm in the kitchen. When I think, "I made dinner, and he can't even bother to answer me or show up?" It can make me really mad! Actually, I've been known to let my thoughts take me into quite a tizzy! By that time my anger is simmering right along with dinner.

Now here's the main thing: You know my mission is to splash God's love and joy. Well, I cannot be splashing when I'm simmering with anger!

Here's how I can put SPACE to work:

<u>S</u>top!

<u>P</u>ause! I take a couple deep breaths to get calm, to stop my spiral of negative thoughts.

<u>A</u>lign with my mission. I want to splash love and joy! I also want to have a close, fun relationship with my husband.

<u>C</u>hoose my response. Instead of reacting in old habitual ways, like yelling to him or at him, I have options.

>*I can think, "Maybe he didn't hear me." I could calmly go downstairs and tell him dinner is ready.

>*Or I could set a time that dinner will be ready, and leave it to him to appear at the scheduled time.

>*I could go ahead and eat dinner without him. (I'm already evaluating that idea: I couldn't enjoy my dinner, and it would probably make him mad. So that option is out.)

>*Or at a time when we are both calm, we could talk about it and come up with a win-win plan.

<u>E</u>valuate my choice. Let's look at a time when I chose to be gracious and give Charlie the benefit of the doubt. I stayed calm, walked downstairs and discovered that he didn't hear me. I tell him dinner is ready, and we have a pleasant dinner and conversation.

Now it's your turn. What stresses you? Causes anxiety? Try creating SPACE. Put the five steps to work. What happens? How does it affect you and the people involved? I'd love to hear your situation, how you flip from old-habit *reaction* to your best-self *response*!

Create a Gap

There's another term for SPACE that Frank Mallinder uses. Frank was one of my first coaches, and he's the author of the book, *Practical Wisdom, A Seeker's Guide to a Meaningful Life.* His term for SPACE is "The gap."

God is in the gap! Whether it's a second or an hour or a day, your power to choose is in that gap, in that SPACE. When you choose your response, you land on your feet – on the solid ground of your best self.

Points to Ponder

1. What are your gems from the Create SPACE chapter?

2. What is an old, habitual way of thinking or feeling that creates stress or anxiety for you?

3. What will you do to create SPACE to be your best self?

Jan Glowe-Janke

Chapter 8

Be the STAR that You Are!

*"We are stars wrapped in skin.
The light you are seeking has always been within."*
-Rumi

My Toastmasters club and my Toasty friends bring me great joy. Presenting a speech – well, not so much. Even after I'd been in the club a few years and had presented many speeches, my fears had a tendency to take over. I could still get myself pretty worked up over the idea of giving a speech.

Finally, I had the brainstorm to apply my coaching techniques to presenting a speech. There's an Ah-Ha moment!

I put SPACE to work:

Stopped (the panic!)

Paused – took a couple deep breaths

Aligned with the joyful part of who God created me to be, and I

Chose to have fun with the speech writing. The following Dr. Seuss-y poem was the result.

Evaluated my choice of action. The poem was a delight to write, and the presentation was enjoyable for my audience. It was actually the beginning of a shift in my thinking about presenting speeches too. I began to think of speaking as an opportunity to pay forward many wonderful things I've learned from a multitude of magnificent teachers.

I renewed my mind!

I created SPACE to take captive the thought that giving speeches puts me in a tizzy – and instead, I chose instead to have fun!

Hopefully, reading the poem will delight you too. Out loud is best. Maybe you'd even consider reading it to your kids or grandkids. You could possibly use it as a teaching tool, but most of all, a shared experience to laugh and enjoy.

Be the Star that You Are!

By Jan Glowe-Janke

If the thought of writing and presenting a speech
    sends you into a tizzy
Or turns you into a bear – maybe even a grizzly . . .
Don't despair! There is something you can do.

No matter the situation
    that triggers unwelcome emotions inside,
No matter who pushes your buttons
    to send your blood pressure sky-high,
Know this: You *can* manage your emotions.
    YOU get to decide.

Decide right now to be the STAR that you are
    with your family, at work and in Toastmasters too.
Know that you can harness your emotions.
    YOU are in control of you!

Know that you're normal
    when unwanted feelings show up.
Notice the feeling. See the red flag.
    Just observe – like a spectator at a game.

There will be times when you feel
    put-out, stressed out, panicky or perturbed,
    neglected, disrespected, worried or unsure.
You may feel disgusted, discouraged, deflated or left out,

regretful, fretful, frightened or full of doubt,
guilty, grumpy, antagonized or mad,
obligated, discombobulated, weary, weak or sad.

Just notice those negative emotions when they appear.
But stand your ground.
Stand firm!
You can look in, but don't build a condo there!

Harness those feelings,
those thieves of confidence and joy.
Remember: YOU are in control of you,
and here's what you can do:

Stop! Pause! Take a deep breath – or two or three.
In that SPACE, that gap,
Choose carefully – what to do, to say, to be.

Renew your mind; chose a loving way to think.
That new thought will *refresh* your spirit
as fast as you can blink.

Don't build your condo in the land of emotional strife;
build it instead where your emotions give you life!

Live where you consistently feel
loving, loveable, loyal and delighted,
peaceful, patient, productive and excited,
passionate enthusiastic, creative and alive,
eager, empowered, equipped and energized.

You have the power to feel
purpose-full, peachy, confident and calm,
helpful, hopeful, healthy, brave and strong,
radiant, resilient, relaxed, refreshed, renewed,
faithful, forgiving, accepting and amused,
connected, protected, kind and dedicated,
grateful – always—to be blessed and highly-favored!

Practice managing your emotions;
you'll get better every day.
Create a gap, create SPACE – it IS the very best way.

You are a star wrapped in skin
growing gloriously into your potential.
Tap into the Light that's glowing within –
so your joy can be exponential!

Jan Glowe-Janke

Chapter 9

Let Go

"One of the happiest moments in life
is when you find the courage
to let go of what you can't change."
-Anonymous

Charlie put a big map of the world in our kitchen, and he gave me a dart. He said, "Throw this dart, Jan, and wherever it lands, I will take you there – when this pandemic is over." I was excitedly thinking Hawaii, the Canary Islands, even Connecticut to visit friends. Well, I threw the dart. Looks like we'll be spending two weeks behind our refrigerator!

That is a funny story I read on Facebook in March, 2020. It was the beginning of the pandemic, the shutdowns and the stay-home orders. It was a time when we all desperately needed to laugh, to lighten up! There was nothing funny going on in our world.

Actually, I laughed really hard at the story about throwing a dart and totally missing the target – it's a topic that hits close to home. We have a group of friends, the Cabin Crew. We spend time together up north; we kayak, play games and laugh a lot.

One of the games we play is Jarts golf. Do you remember Jarts? They've probably been taken off the market because they're so dangerous. Those wickedly sharp, pointy ends can do a lot of damage. Well, I developed a reputation for Jart-throwing, and it's not particularly a good one. When it's my turn to throw, my friends scramble for cover – for good reason!

I've been known to throw Jarts that have stabbed trees, stuck in the roof and splashed into the river. The scariest Jart I've ever thrown soared over my head and landed behind me. The problem seems to be that I'm not good at letting go.

Jarts are not the only thing I've had trouble letting go. I've held on to old wounds and regrets. I've held on to expectations of myself and of others. I've held on to a desire for others to change. I've even held on to certain people when clearly it wasn't healthy. Too many times, not letting go kept me as stuck as that Jart in the roof. And holding on hurts.

Can you relate? Is there something you want to let go? Need to let go? What holds you back from being the best version of yourself? What do you tend to worry about? Think of old hurts, disappointments, doubts, fears and frustrations that tromp around in your head and steal your joy.

Just imagine how freeing it would be to let go – let go of worry, worrying about what others think, worrying about what has happened or what might happen. Those worries are fears, and we *can* let them go. Imagine how letting go would soothe your soul.

When we keep calm, create a space, pause and listen to our hearts, we know. Knowing what to let go and when to let go is essential for our joy.

Let Go of Worry

"Worry about tomorrow steals the joy from today."
-Barbara Cameron

Worry can be a habit. It was for me.

My mom was a worrier. She'd say, "If I worry about it, it won't happen." As you can imagine, I learned from her example. And I worried about everything from what clothes to wear to who might die, and everything imaginable in between.

I used to worry myself into being mad, and I could even worry myself into being sick. If it was late at night, and Charlie wasn't home from working at a track meet (even when I knew he'd be late), I'd be worried that he'd been in an accident and was lying in a ditch somewhere. By the time he got home, I had fretted so much and worked myself into such a tizzy that I'd be really angry at him. Even as I write this, it sounds ridiculous! It was an old, habitual way of thinking that was not only stealing my joy, it was making me sick to my stomach and hurting our relationship. Thankfully, God sent me help.

In the teachers' lounge at lunch one day, we were talking about things we'd learned from our moms. I wasn't the only one who had the learned the worry habit. Our librarian said quietly, "Worrying is an insult to God." That Truth took my breath away like a slap in the face. It was a wake-up call. As I walked down the hallway I prayed, "God, I absolutely do not want to insult you by worrying. Please help me!" And talking to God was a new thing for me.

That was early in my walk with God (I was in my 40s). I had just started listening to Family Life Radio. In the very same week I had prayed for help, I heard a radio program that changed my thinking. The message was, "Turn your worry into a prayer."

> *"Turn your worry*
> *into a prayer."*

So instead of thinking about Charlie being in an accident, I started praying, *"God, thank you for taking good care of Charlie and bringing him home safely."*

Often when we want to know how to do something, we grab our phones and search the web. We have another resource at our fingertips. The very best instruction manual is the Bible. (A convenient place to tap into many translations is https://www.biblegateway.com)

Not surprisingly, Scripture offers a how-not-to-worry recipe.

"Don't fret or worry. Instead of worrying, pray. Let petitions and praises shape your worries into prayers, letting God know your concerns. Before you know it, a sense of God's wholeness, everything coming together for good, will come and settle you down. It's wonderful what happens when Christ displaces worry at the center of your life."

Philippians 4: 6, 7 MSG

A Process to Free Yourself from Worry

1. Pray -- tell God your concerns.

2. Pray with thanksgiving.

3. Settle down; know and feel God's peace that transcends all understanding.

He already knows what we are concerned about, but he loves it when we bring our cares to him. Scripture tells us to pray with thanksgiving, maybe because thanksgiving transforms our hearts and our minds. Feeling grateful softens us. Settling down, breathing, being calm will put us into his presence so we can feel his peace. Sometimes, it might only take a minute to get there; sometimes settling down will take longer. We would be wise to "stay there till we get there."

"Your strength will come from settling down in complete dependence on me."

Isaiah 30:15 MSG

101

Mary and Wendell's Story

COVID 19 closed the border between the United States and Canada. That was a problem, a big problem, for Mary and Wendell. They live in southern Michigan and have a second home in Canada on Lake Superior, four hundred miles away. They have been trying to sell their Canadian home for two years because it is getting too difficult to keep up two homes.

Their realtor had tried to show it a month earlier. The door lock was jammed, and she couldn't get in to show it. She wanted to show it again, but she was afraid she wouldn't be able to get in.

Mary tried calling the Border Patrol to see if they could cross in an emergency situation, but they were not accepting calls. Mary and Wendell were at their wits' end to figure it out. It was a very stressful time for both of them.

They do daily devotions and pray together a lot, but this situation called for them to lean more heavily upon God. Mary said, "We know we have to trust him to work things out in his own time, but we felt desperate. We prayed for a closer walk with him. We also asked God to relieve our anxiety. We know in our minds that we need to trust more, but putting that into practice during a difficult situation is a different story. We learned a very valuable lesson that day and feel confident that God will work all this to our good. Trusting in him and handing him our problems is the best solution."

Mary and Wendell talk to God like they talk to a friend. They told God their concerns and they trusted him for a solution. Did you notice how they also asked God to relieve their anxiety? And how they prayed for a closer walk with him? We can do that too.

Let Go of Fears

I recently saw the movie, *Harriet*, which is about Harriet Tubman. She is an incredible example of one who talked to God and settled into his peace – in spite of terrifying circumstances. Her peace gives us a picture of "peace that transcends understanding."

In the movie when Harriet first runs away, she talks with a pastor. He warns her, "You will face many dangers – copperheads, wolves and hunger. But," he tells her, "Your worst enemy is FEAR."

Harriet prayed continually. She never prayed to be delivered from dangerous circumstances. She was solely focused on God and her mission to lead slaves to freedom. Harriet's purpose infused her with incredible courage, supernatural courage. She kept calm. She continually turned to God for direction. She prayed for strength. Harriet found *everything* she needed in the presence of God.

Everything you and I need can be found in God's presence too. He is with us always, and he is an ever-present help in trouble. (Psalm 46:1) As we become aware of the fear we want to let go, and pray with thanksgiving, we can know and feel God's peace.

Points to Ponder

1. What are your gems from the Let Go chapter?

2. Identify a worry or fear God is nudging you to let go.

3. What will you do to let go of that worry or fear?

Chapter 10

Shake It Off

"Sometimes you have to let go of the picture of what you thought it would be like and learn to find joy in the story you are actually living."

-Rachel Marie Martin

Refrain from Ruminating

Let's say you've had a wonderful day. You had a peaceful quiet time in the morning, you had great conversations with your favorite people, you accomplished goals, and you laughed with a friend. You also had a disagreement with a co-worker. When you lay your head on your pillow at night, what do you think about?

Of course, the one negative event of the day will most likely be hopping around in your head.

That's called rumination; to focus on bad experiences and feelings from the past. Ruminating re-triggers negative emotions, and that stimulates stress.

Ruminating is a normal human response. For most of us, ruminating has most likely become a habitual way of thinking. The good news is we don't have to keep ruminating. Our job is to simply notice when we are being swept onto the train of rumination; that awareness empowers us. We can choose to hop off that train of negativity and jump on a different one. Let's jump on the train that will take us where we want to go— joy is our destination. The train of blessings and gratitude will help us get to our good cheer.

🐾🐾🐾🐾🐾🐾🐾

When I was going through a divorce, I was devastated. I totally lost my joy. I couldn't quit thinking about how betrayed I felt. Since it was all I thought about, it was pretty much all I talked about. Not much fun for people who loved me!

A few months after my husband left, I continued to dwell on the negative. I visited my parents. I was grumbling and complaining, still crazy-mad about it all. Mom, with her typical love and wisdom, said gently, "Honey, we know you're hurting. Maybe it would be a good idea if you only talked to us about it." She knew I was making myself – and others – miserable by constantly talking about it to everyone who would listen. My ruminating was keeping the hurt alive.

What in the world would make me want to keep re-living the pain? Maybe at that point I didn't realize I had a choice, that there really was a better way to get through those rough waters. Or maybe I just chose, consciously or unconsciously, to continue thinking and acting like a victim. I had dug myself into a rut, and I certainly needed help. At that time I didn't know God. Now I know Scripture offers a solution, a lifeline.

> *"Forget the former things; do not dwell on the past.*
> *See, I am doing a new thing!*
> *Now it springs up; do you not perceive it?*
> *I am making a way in the desert*
> *and streams in the wasteland."*
>
> Isaiah 43:18, 19 NIV

Instead of Ruminating, We Can . . .

1. Pray with Faith and Gratitude

"Lord, help me forget the former things and not dwell on the past. Help me let go of the pain. I give you all my hurts. Thank you that you work all things for good. Please give me eyes to see the new things you are doing. And help me hold onto hope. Thank you that you are a Way-Maker, and that with you, all things are possible. Amen"

2. Look for the New Things God Is Doing

"God says that He is actively looking for someone to be good to . . . But he cannot pour out his goodness on anyone who has a negative attitude. He is looking for someone who is on the lookout all the time, someone who is full of faith and trust, someone who is eagerly anticipating his gracious gifts. He wants to be good to you, so be expecting an outpouring of His goodness!" [13]

3. *Start a New Habit ~ Tonight*

When you put your head on your pillow, observe your thoughts. Remember, it is natural for our brains to dwell on the negative. You are choosing to make a change – to hop off the train of rumination. You are choosing to hop onto the train that will take you to your joy.

Think of highlights of your day. Reflect on the things that made you smile. Ponder the people who encouraged you and the activities that energized you. Think about your blessings, and let gratitude fill your heart.

Depending on what is happening in your life, you may have to make the choice to jump off the train of rumination two or three times. There may be some nights that require making that choice 222 times. It's all fine – no criticizing, no judging ourselves as we move toward a new perspective. When you've boarded the Gratitude and Good Cheer Train, bask in the beauty and the blessings, linger in the love.

Shake It Off

What I'm about to tell you may sound a little weird. If I hadn't spent so many years in yoga classes, I'd think it was pretty strange too. Now I know that even though it's unusual, it feels pretty good, and it works. Here's an idea to get you thinking in the direction I'm going: Let's say a fly lands on your shoulder. What do you do? You would flick it off; right?

Now let's say something that's bigger and creepier is on your shoulder. For me that would be a big, furry spider or something snake-y. So I'd quickly brush it off, then I'd have to do something more drastic to get rid of the feel of the critter.

Picture a dog swimming. What happens the minute he gets out of the water? Yes, he shakes it off! Actually, my friend and yoga teacher Jeanette says that shaking is a natural part of the animal kingdom. Particularly after a traumatic event, an animal must literally shake off its fear response before they can get back to living in the moment. Jeanette believes the old saying, "Your tissues hold your issues." She says, "Muscle contraction and release are vital for the nervous system to regulate and settle. Shaking helps the body release its pent-up responses to stress."

Do you have pent-up emotions you want to release? Stress or issues you want to shake off? Let's give it a try. You can start with shaking your hands. Use a flicking motion like you just washed your hands and can't find a towel to dry them. Try closing your eyes or not, whichever feels better. You can let your arms hang at your sides and shake them. Stand with your feet hip-width apart and try bouncing at your knees. Soften your shoulders and swing your arms till you feel like the scarecrow in *The Wizard of Oz*. You can even hum as you shake. Feel the release. After a minute or two or five, stop. Notice the tingling and the flow of energy in your body. You've just given yourself a gift of release. Take time to relax and enjoy the refreshment you created.

Think of fears or feelings you want to shake off. Let's go right to the big one, the one you're apt to ruminate on. Got it in mind? Maybe even write it down. Now hold that thought while you read the next story.

The Donkey in the Well

One day a farmer's donkey fell down into a well. The poor donkey cried and cried for hours as the farmer tried to figure out what to do. Finally he decided that the animal was old, and the well needed to be covered up anyway. It just wasn't worth it to save the donkey.

The farmer invited all his neighbors to come over and help him. They all grabbed a shovel and began to shovel dirt into the well. At first the donkey panicked. He cried horribly. Then, to everyone's amazement, he quieted down. A few shovel loads later, the farmer was astonished at what he saw.

With each shovel full of dirt that hit his back, the donkey would shake it off and step up. Shake it off and step up, next shovel full of dirt, the donkey would shake it off and step up.

Pretty soon everyone was astounded to see the donkey step up over the edge of the well and happily trot off.

What the donkey thought would bury him actually turned out to bless him! He shook off the dirt, stepped up and got out of the well.

You and I have had situations like that. We've felt like we're being buried. But when we keep calm, we can think clearly. We can see opportunities.

Recall that issue you tend to ruminate on. Look for the blessing, the lesson in it. How can it make you stronger or better? How might it put you in a position to help someone else? Those uplifting thoughts carry us through rough waters. They keep us moving forward. They help us be of good cheer.

Let go,
shake it off and step up!

Points to Ponder

1. What are your gems from the Shake It Off chapter?

2. What are the issues and/or feelings you tend to ruminate on? How might it be a blessing in disguise?

3. What will you do to step up and be the best version of yourself?

Chapter 11

Feed Your Faith

"Feed your faith and your fears will starve to death."
-Anonymous

Two Wolves

A grandfather is teaching his grandson about life. The grandfather says, "A fight is going on inside me, and it's a terrible fight. It's between two wolves. One is evil: it is anger, envy, greed, sorrow, regret, arrogance, resentment, self-pity, false pride, superiority, ego, inferiority, fear.

The other wolf is good. It is joy, peace, love, hope, serenity, humility, kindness, empathy, generosity, truth, compassion, self-control, faith."

Grandfather tells the boy, "The same fight is going on inside you and inside every other person too."

The grandson thinks for a minute, and he asks, "Grandfather, which wolf will win?"

The grandfather simply replies, "The one you feed."

Feeding your faith is about feeding the right wolf, and that's a lot like having a good healthy diet, a diet that is much more than what we put into our mouths. It is everything you "take in" – what you watch, what you read, what you listen to. The people you hang around with. It is everything you "let in" to your mind, body and spirit.

Feeding the right wolf and starving the evil wolf can shift us from grumpy to grateful, from self-pity to praise, from fear to faith.

How Modern-Day Saints Feed Their Faith

*"May the God of hope fill you with all joy
and peace as you trust in him . . ."*

Romans 15:13 NIV

To trust someone, you have to know that someone.

Many of my friends get to know God better, purpose-fully. Let me introduce you to Laura, Michelle, Robin, Wendy and Judy. They engage in intentional practices that keep them grounded in God. They are faith-filled, peaceful and strong. Each one has agreed to share a peek into her/his intimate relationship with God.

Laura

"I've learned that I have to have at least 30 minutes of 'me' time every day so my faith can be fed. (More if I'm lucky – we American women are *busy*– so sad but true we need to carve out time for ourselves.)

What feeds my faith is acknowledging and thanking God daily for the blessings he has given me. It is conscientiously looking for good:

> Found a great parking spot at work? Thank God.

> Enjoying the warm breeze blowing across my face as I sit alone in my back yard under a 100-year-old oak? Thank God.

> Had a family get together and everyone actually got along? Thank God.

> Someone pulled out in front of me and then proceeded to drive slowly and then turn left? Thank God for the grace of not honking my horn or giving any un-Christian like gestures.

> Difficult co-worker? Thank God for closing my mouth until I can think of an appropriate response.

On the flip side when I screw up, I admit my issues to God and ask Him for wisdom and guidance to do better the next time. Or how to make amends this time. We have someone who is all-mighty, all-knowing and *perfect*, and he still loves me. How awesome is that?

The God who made this universe just by speaking is willing to listen to me whenever I want. He knows the good, the bad and the ugly about Laura, and he still loves me and wants a relationship with me."

Laura intentionally feeds her faith daily, weekly and monthly:

1) "I read a chapter of the Bible usually every day. (This takes about 5-10 minutes.)

2) I spend 30 minutes of quiet 'me' time every day – walking or reading a book (usually fiction).

3) I actively look for ways to praise God. I hang out with a group of friends who also love God. We meet monthly and discuss our lives and pray for each other. It is awesome.

4) I attend church or listen to a sermon online usually weekly."

Michelle

"When I spend quiet time with God, it is usually first thing in the morning. I grab my notebook/sketchpad and my Bible and head for my prayer closet, a.k.a. my bedroom. I use my notebook to journal my prayers and conversation with God.

I begin my time with the Lord by either saying the Lord's Prayer or asking if there is a specific devotional he would like me to read, and just see where he leads me. He will sometimes bring song lyrics to mind, so I will listen to that song, and he speaks through it, or sometimes it is a Bible verse or a random sermon online.

Sometimes I just ask him questions like,

> ➤ Lord, what do you want me to know today?

> ➤ What do you want me to pick up or lay down?

> ➤ God, what do you want love to look like through me today?

> ➤ Father, who are you making me now?

The goal is always putting God in his rightful first place in my heart and day, totally surrendering, by laying everything and everyone at his feet, and then opening my heart to hear his powerful and loving voice guide me through the Holy Spirit . . . it fills me to overflowing and makes me ready for another day.

I've become so dependent on him and this morning time together, I cannot imagine trying to do life without it. It is how I live, move and have my being. (Acts 17:28) There is absolutely no joy like it on earth."

Robin

For years, Robin has enjoyed an early morning quiet time, several days a week. He feeds his faith by reading. Following a yearly plan, he is reading through the Bible chronologically. His favorite faith-feeding books are *Draw the Circle, the 40-Day Prayer Challenge* by Mark Batterson, *The Prayer Powered Entrepreneur* by Kim Avery, and John Ortberg's books. Another book he really liked is Paul Miller's *A Praying Life*.

Robin says, "My wife and I spend about 20 minutes in the evening reading a devotion book. That gives us time to wind down, pray and get in sync. As I'm reading, when something strikes me, I write it down in my planner; that has become my journal."

Part of Robin's quiet time is writing what he's grateful for. I asked, "How do you do that for all these years? Do you write the same things over and over again?"

Robin replied, "I want to be grateful for what *will* happen even though I don't know what that is." (*Now that's trust!*) For example, "I am grateful for the women I work with. Let me be the leader they need today."

Wendy

"What if I can't find quiet time?" Wendy asked herself the question many years ago; it's a question that may be on your mind too. She is now a seasoned woman of faith and prayer, and she teaches a workshop, "Personal Quiet Time, How to Begin." I'll skim the surface of her teachings for you, after we look at how she began:

"I was married; I had four daughters, ages nine, seven, six and two and a half. I was also working part time. At various times I would be successful with quiet times, for a while. Then it would fall by the wayside. My frustrations were mostly with time. How in the world could I fit in one more thing? One day I received in the mail a brochure entitled, *7 Minutes with God; How to Plan a Daily Quiet Time.* I thought, even I can spare seven minutes. And just like exercise, that's how I finally got started.

My husband bought me a rocker just before our first daughter was born. It's a special spot. It's near the front window of our house which is a bow window that has a built-in shelf. That's important because I need somewhere to set my coffee. I have a basket next to the rocker where I keep my Bible. So, it's always there waiting for me. My special spot calls out to me to come and relax."

Wendy's basic outline for quiet time

1. Pray for guidance and ask God to meet with me (½ minute)
2. Read the Bible (4 minutes)
3. Pray using A-C-T-S (2 ½ minutes) [14]

   Adoration (praise and worship)

   Confession

   Thanksgiving

   Supplication

"Every day that I meet with God, I pray for my children and husband using the *Power of Praying* books. I *love* these books." (Wendy is referring to Stormie Omartian's books, including *Power of a Praying Wife* and *Power of a Praying Parent.*)

As a foundation, Wendy teaches: "It's important to establish a *habit* of quiet time. 1) Find a quiet spot and use the same spot each time. 2) Do it regularly, *whatever that honestly means for you.* 3) Determine what tools (books, devotionals) you will use for Bible reading. 4) Develop a system of highlighting or making notations. 5) Consider keeping a journal.

What if I can't find a quiet time? Well, we all lead busy lives, and there will be days that don't have a quiet moment in them. On those days I try to meet with the Lord however I can. I may not have time to read the Bible, but I can listen to Family Life Radio or praise and worship music. I can have a *loud* time of worship as I work around the house or drive in the car, and I can pray as I drive or walk. I can listen to the Bible or Christian speakers on podcasts.

God likes to hear about everything that's going on in our lives, not because he doesn't know if we don't tell him, but because he loves the relationship with us. The conversation. When I arrive at my destination safely, I thank him. When I am struggling for patience, I ask him. When I'm worried about something, I tell him.

We may not be able to have the perfect quiet time each day, but we can make substitution and do the best we can."

Ask a "Saint" to Mentor You

Seven minutes of quiet time each day was the first suggestion from my spiritual mentor. Before I tell you the abundant blessings of having a mentor, I need to tell you how it all happened.

A friend invited me to her church. I had gone to church regularly as a kid, but then there was a big gap of time – over 25 years. I was in my 40s when I went to church with my friend, and I liked it. A lot. The people were friendly, the sermons were relevant, and I was searching. Something was missing in my heart, my life.

In church I met Judy. Her joyful spirit was a magnet. I was mesmerized by her smile, her radiance, her reverence and warmth. I always tried to sit near her, and we talked a little each Sunday.

One morning after the service, Judy and I were talking. I hardly knew her, so imagine my shock, when out of my mouth flew the request, "Would you be my spiritual mentor?" That thought had never crossed my mind! But the question rolled out, and there it sat. And there we sat. It was very quiet. A tear trickled down Judy's cheek, then another. "What?" I thought.

She said quietly, "I'd love to mentor you, Jan." Wouldn't you know – she had just finished a class, training to be a mentor! And so it began.

We met an hour each week for a year. With Judy as my mentor, I learned practical life-changing, joy-increasing, faith-building lessons.

Three Lifelines from my Spiritual Mentor

1) *Have seven minutes of quiet time with God every day*

Read the Bible. Get to know him. Talk to him and listen to him. Learn about him.

2) *Figure out what you want*

Judy asked me, "What do you want, Jan?" And she kept asking the question to help me get to the answers within me. That question was the second life-line she threw me.

When I retired, I promised myself, "No schedule for a year!" As a teacher and a school counselor, my life had been run by the clock, bells, my lesson plan book and my calendar – for decades. Maybe you can understand the desire to *not* have a schedule? Have you ever tried living without a schedule? Well, let me tell you how my life with *no* schedule worked . . . It didn't!

For everything – that birthday card, that cleaning project, that visit to friends and relatives, even that party – I had the mindset, "I can do that tomorrow." As you can imagine, nothing got done. Not only did I not accomplish anything, I didn't have any passion – or joy. Finally, I had an epiphany. My life without a schedule wasn't working because I was focused on what I *didn't* want!

While it's good to know what we *don't* want, we need to know what we *really do want*.

When it came right down to it, my true desire was to *choose the activities* of my days and to engage in those activities *when* I chose. Finally, I began to figure it out. What I wanted was time for prayer, reading and exercise. I wanted time for the people and projects that refresh me and bring me joy.

I'd heard that "Whatever we focus on expands." So I began to focus on what I wanted.

3) *Implement the "Good Day Practice"*

Charlie was experiencing some serious health issues, and I was pretty unsettled. Judy came to my rescue with what she calls the "Good Day Practice." Having this simple, two-part plan, even a skeleton of a schedule, turned out to be the anchor I needed then, and one of the best things I still do to center and refresh myself.

Here's an explanation of the Good Day Practice. I use a small 4"x6" notebook from the Dollar Store. Mine has a "Choose Joy" cover. Some of my friends use index cards.

Part One ~ In the morning I write these headings on a page in my notebook:

➢ *Spirit*

➢ *Mind*

➢ *Body*

➢ *Service*

➢ *Fun*

Then I write *one thing* (just one!) in each category I will do that day. Judy says, "Think of each item you write as a promise to yourself." I'll share some of my examples:

➢ *Spirit:* Read a daily devotional from Sarah Young's *Jesus Calling* or watch a sermon online

> *Mind:* Listen to a Professional Christian Coaching Today podcast *or* read a Blue Zones newsletter *or* watch an inspirational TED Talk

> *Body:* Walk outside for 45 minutes *or* do 30 minutes of yoga *or* yoqi *or* plant flowers

> *Service:* Call Aunt Wilma *or* host my Monday morning Splash Call (those fit the *fun* category too!) *or* write a sympathy card *or* write a thank you note

> *Fun:* Meet Sue for a walk *or* watch a movie with Charlie *or* sit in my swing and read

Part Two ~ Gratitude

Write five to ten things I am grateful for. (Once I get going, it's hard to stop at ten!)

> I am grateful this book is written and published and that *you* are reading it!

> I am grateful to Sam Horn for her gift of fabulous daily teachings on Facebook, "So, You Want to Write a Book."

> I am grateful to my brother, Rick, for surprising me with his generous gift of a flute! (I hadn't played in 50 years!)

> I am grateful that the guys working on the neighbor's house next to my office window finally turned their radio off!

➢ I am grateful for Brad, our son-in-law; he is a devoted husband and dad. He has great passion for God and America. He is always grateful, and he says so!

➢ I am grateful to Debby and Mac for generously sharing their cabin and toys, for decades.

➢ I am grateful to Steve and Dawn at Pro Tech Computers in Jackson, Michigan, for rescuing us when we had computer problems, and making it easy and affordable.

➢ I am grateful to the dedicated people who lovingly serve in our church and in the community.

➢ I am grateful to Charlie's family for embracing me with open arms – and that they like to play games!

➢ I am grateful for my friend Sue; she's an inspiration for health and happiness. Her yoga classes and Ayurveda wisdom make me healthier. I'm energized by our walks and talks and laughs, and comforted by her prayers for my family and me.

🌰🌰🌰🌰🌰🌰🌰

A personal quiet time is all about getting in God's presence, and it's about the fullness of joy available to us in his presence (Psalm 16:11).

Laura, Michelle, Robin, Wendy and Judy know that they are God's children and he lavishes love on them (1 John 3:1).

They know that everything they need is in his presence (Philippians 4:19).

They know that God is with them always (Joshua 1: 9), and they trust him. They trust his love, his timing and his ways.

And they are grateful.

They crave quiet time with God; it feeds their faith and starves their doubts and fears. Their faith empowers, enlivens and equips them, and it gives them joy for the journey.

Points to Ponder

1. What are your gems from the Feed Your Faith chapter?

2. What is one negative that you will diminish or eliminate? How will you starve the evil wolf?

3. What will you do to feed the right wolf?

4. What do you want? Journal your thoughts about what you want. Talk with a friend or coach about it. (Your *true* desires are placed in your heart by God.)

5. List several people whose faith you admire. Consider asking God to show you which person to ask to mentor you. Then ask.

Jan Glowe-Janke

Chapter 12

Celebrate Resilience

"Joy collected over time fuels resilience."
-Brené Brown

What does resilience have to do with joy?

Resilience is like a bungee cord; it always bounces back. There is energy and liveliness in that bounce. There is no joy in staying stuck, stretched out, being grumpy, and there's no joy in self-pity or in giving up. Tessa Bielecki writes about the resilience of the saints and mystics; she calls resilience "the bounce that counts."

I am excited and so honored to introduce you to three dear friends. They are modern-day saints who know rough waters. They have been tossed about by turbulence that would threaten to throw the strongest among us out of the boat, maybe even drown us. They have overcome rejection, failure, abuse and health challenges. And they adapt; they bounce back.

How do they do that?

As you read about Mickie, Melissa and Mark, you will see qualities conducive to their resilience. In each of them you'll see an amazing will, an unquenchable Spirit, to press on. They bounce back -- and more. They *become* better and stronger on the other side of struggles.

Mickie

Mickie was always the new kid, always had to figure out where she fit in. By the time she was in eighth grade she'd been the new kid in seven different schools. Between her freshman and sophomore years her family was moving again. Mickie was tired of not fitting in. She remembers thinking, "Nobody knows me. I can be whatever I want."

So she marched into that new school with a whole new attitude. She auditioned for a play and was chosen as the lead dancer. She tried out for cheerleading. She was placed in an Honors English Class. At first she thought, "I don't belong here." (A counselor in a previous school had told Mickie she wasn't smart enough to go to college. She advised Mickie to be a cosmetologist or get married.) But Mickie decided to stay in the honors class, and to her surprise, she did well. It was Mickie's best year ever.

By the time she graduated, Mickie was engaged to Mike. She was saving tip money for her wedding cake, and she'd hidden the money. When it disappeared, she knew her brothers had stolen it for drugs. Her mom said, "You shouldn't have put the money where they could find it." Mickie heard the unspoken messages, "You're not as valuable as the boys," and "Negative behavior of men is acceptable; make excuses for them; protect them."

It's not a surprise that the man Mickie chose to marry was abusive. It's what she knew. It felt normal. She thought keeping her husband between the lines was her responsibility. And she got really good at pretending everything was okay when it wasn't. Three times she left him; three times she went back. It would be nine more years before she finally left for good. (Mickie has written about it in her book, *Looking behind Closed Doors*.)

Mickie knew she had to change herself or she'd go back to him again . . . or marry someone else who was abusive. She didn't trust herself to date.

Her solution? She put herself "in the repair shop."

"I needed to change me. That isn't free, and I didn't have any money. I got a low limit credit card and paid it off every month. A credit card is like a rope – It can hang you or pull you out of the mud. I bought books, took classes, and hired coaches." Mickie knew it wouldn't be easy, but she was determined to break the pattern.

She really values those five years of personal growth in the repair shop. She learned to let go. Mickie says, "I was angry for many years. While I was still married, we moved to California and I didn't talk to my parents. Now I realize they did the best they could. You can't be resilient if you hold onto hurts and anxiety."

Finally, Mickie felt like she could turn to God. She had spent years being atheist, then agnostic. Mickie recalls a turning point during her marriage which she now recognizes as Divine Intervention. When her son was a baby, an insurance salesman came to her door. He said, "I only sell life insurance to people who are saved." Mickie ordered him off her porch! But the next day she went to the store and bought a Bible. She read it cover to cover. She read in the mornings, in secret, because her husband thought all religion was a crutch. (He didn't like Mickie taking college classes or having friends either.)

While she was in the repair shop, Mickie said to God, "Here I am. Do what you need to do." She had spent years hating Mike. Now she knows he's on his path; she's on hers. She had to learn to forgive him. And she had to forgive herself.

With God's help Mickie changed herself -- and that changed everything. She broke the pattern; she let go of old mindsets that kept her bound. Over the past 15 years I've known her, Mickie has blossomed. The names of her coaching businesses illustrate her transformations:

- ➢ Test the Strength of the Rope
- ➢ The 2nd 53 Years (Mickie intends to live to be 106. The first 53 years were for someone else; the 2nd 53 years are for being her authentic self.)
- ➢ Figuring It out after 50
- ➢ Shatterproof
- ➢ Cool Retired Women Community

Remember when Mickie started at a new school as a sophomore, and she decided to make it her best year ever?

Turns out her boyfriend from that year found her – decades later! They started talking on the phone, daily. They re-connected, fell in love again, and now they are married. Mickie's story is a "happy ever after" story.

Mickie fully accepts her past, she continues to take responsibility for her joy, and she embraces her God-given purpose, to be a beacon. Her resilient Spirit has taken her from surviving to thriving – radiantly!

Melissa

She always has a warm smile and a compassionate, listening ear. She is light and lively. She laughs easily. She has a child-like innocence, a gentleness and graciousness, a purity of Spirit that is magnetic.

That's hardly the description you'd expect of someone who has been haunted by a feeling of failure and rejection, someone who was diagnosed with cancer at age 30, and someone who has struggled with depression. How can she be so sweet, kind and consistently cheerful?

One of Melissa's favorite mantras is from the movie, *The Sound of Music*.

> ### *"When God closes a door,*
> ### *somewhere he opens a window."*

So many times in her life, doors have been slammed shut. Looking back, she can see God's hand, always opening a window.

Melissa earned excellent grades; school and homework were her passions. She *loves* to learn. After high school she wasn't sure what to do. She applied to an accelerated combination undergraduate/medical school program that could be completed in six years. She thought, "If I get in, that's what I'm supposed to do." She got in!

For the first three years, Melissa studied intensely. Humanities classes were her favorites, but the hard-core science classes were difficult. She struggled academically. And she struggled emotionally. "I should be able to do this" was the "should" refrain that haunted her. Melissa began to crumble.

At the end of her junior year, she was summoned to appear before a board of professors, students and program administrators. After some very uncomfortable discussion where Melissa tried to plead her case, the spokesperson concluded, "It is evident to us that you are not able to perform this coursework. It is our decision that you will not be allowed to continue in the program."

"Suddenly I was no longer a medical student. My self-esteem was shattered. It was beyond humiliating." Her parents were heartbroken that she wouldn't be a doctor, and that deepened her shame and pain. Now what?

The easiest way to finish her bachelor's degree was to change her major to psychology. As if her academic failure wasn't enough, Melissa's first significant romantic relationship ended. She was devastated. Her whole identity was shaken. Her dreams were demolished. She couldn't stop crying. She experienced her first episode of depression, although she did not realize it at the time.

Melissa sought out a Bible study because she loves to learn and grow in self-awareness. She didn't want to feel pushed into religion, and she had misgivings about certain Christian concepts. Melissa had conversations with new friends in the group who helped her see things from a different perspective. Melissa made a decision to follow God. She says, "I made a purposeful choice to let him have the driver's seat in my life, trusting him and his timing to resolve the philosophical concerns I was struggling with."

Still struggling with depression, Melissa sought counseling. For over a year and a half, she met weekly with her counselor, a lady who was like a spiritual mom to her. *"It's a process,"* was her counselor's mantra. But Melissa was impatient. "People like me who are perfectionists think we should be able to figure things out right away. Eventually I realized just because I can grasp something mentally doesn't mean it will change me psychologically right away. Heart changes usually take time."

It was the beginning of a whole new life for Melissa. She says, "I did so much healing psychologically and spiritually." With help, she began to learn how to trust God and to remodel her distorted thinking, especially about herself. She started to count on God's view of her, even when circumstances are sad or scary. She learned that healthy self-esteem means not worrying so much about what others think. And eventually, she even learned she had to give up trying to please her mom which had been so exhausting. Melissa says, "It hasn't been a nice linear process. Pastor Chuck Swindoll used to say our growth happens in 'three steps forward, two steps back.' Over time, God was slowly but surely renewing my mind."

After a few years, Melissa met and married Tim, who was also a part of her healing. She loved his sister and brothers and their spouses; she felt accepted and understood. She had begun to find her right tribe.

After Melissa and Tim had been married for two years, she was diagnosed with breast cancer; she was just 30 years old. She prayed for complete healing, but she also prayed, "Lord, help me to trust you in this even if you choose not to heal me." Melissa had surgery, six months of chemotherapy and seven weeks of radiation followed by two years of medication. From the beginning, she decided to tell friends about the cancer. "I was honest about the hard things," Melissa says. "I needed to process the issues, so I gave them permission to talk about it. I helped them to help me."

After all of Melissa's cancer treatment was completed, she and Tim chose to pursue parenthood. "It was a difficult decision," she says. "What if my cancer came back?" But she knew if her cancer did not recur, and she got to be fifty years old, she would regret the decision not to have children. "I decided I could not live the rest of my life in fear." Many years later, she is grateful she made that choice because she and Tim now have two wonderful adult daughters.

About the same time Melissa's younger daughter was born, God provided another important support system. Melissa joined a group of girlfriends who met weekly to share prayer requests and support each other. Melissa says, "We needed it weekly because we all had little kids, so life was pretty stressful. God used that group in so many ways. The atmosphere was really safe psychologically, so we could really 'let our hair down.' We learned from each other how to parent, and we all grew spiritually. Some of the women in the group have also struggled with depression, and I felt supported when I finally made the decision to take an anti-depressant medication for a while. We also helped each other with physical needs like babysitting and post-partum meals and even financial needs. That group has been the best example I've ever seen of how the church is truly meant to function. We have really been 'Jesus with skin on' to each other all these years."

Melissa reflects with gratitude at the closed doors in her life. She speaks in awe of how God used "failure," rejection, depression and cancer as opened windows to draw her close to him.

Melissa looks for and expects God's goodness. She expects him to give beauty for ashes, strength for fear, gladness for mourning, and peace for despair (Isaiah 61:3) even if she can't see it right away. She is captivated by the beautiful, creative ways God works, and she knows our hardest times are often when we can see most clearly the beautiful patterns in his tapestry.

🐾🐾🐾🐾🐾🐾🐾

Mark

Mark loved putt-putt golf. His dad had been teaching him the stance, grip and swing. He was really excited when his dad took him to the real putt-putt golf course. Mark's dad carried him as they played the first four holes. On the fifth hole, with his dime store golf clubs, two and a half-year-old Mark stood, leaned back against his dad's legs for support and lined up his putt. He hit a good shot and took off after it. Mark walked the rest of the 18 holes. Mark walked – It was a miracle! It was the first time he had ever walked by himself.

To truly understand the miracle of Mark walking, you need to know how he came into this world.

Doctors told his parents he wouldn't live. You see, when he was born his knees were tucked up into his chest. His feet were wrapped around his neck, and his feet were completely turned around. He had dislocated hips. His hands were deformed. He had one lung and only part of the second lung. He had no sucking, gag or swallow reflex. Right away medical staff put Mark in casts. His arms were in casts from below his elbows to his fingers; his legs were in casts from his knees down and over his feet.

Everyday Sue and David went to the hospital to see their first-born son. Their priest visited Mark in the hospital. Afterwards he talked to Mark's parents. "Do you realize how bad your son is? It might not be good for him to live." Sue didn't know how to pray. Finally, she said, "Lord, your will be done."

Three times that night, doctors gave up on Mark. But one doctor saw signs of life. Sue said, "After that prayer, Mark was not only alive, but he kept improving. He never went downhill, but it was a long, tough climb."

An orthopedic doctor put baby Mark in a body cast. It wrapped around his forehead and down his back. In the front, the cast went from under his armpits down to mid-thigh. And it was working. Straightened out by the cast, Mark could swallow and suck and gag.

Once the doctors figured out how to put hinges and buckles on the cast, they could bring Mark home. Another miracle! He was four months old before they could hold him, and even then he was encased in solid plaster.

When Mark was two years old his parents took him to physical therapy sponsored by Easter Seals five days a week; that was their routine for two years.

From second grade on, Mark attended regular schools and earned good grades. He was a voracious reader. Summers for Mark meant many surgeries for many reasons. Some of the surgeries involved taking tendons from his toes and putting them in his thumbs. Those surgeries enabled Mark to use his hands; now he could hold a pencil and grip a golf club.

During those times in hospitals and recovering, Mark became a sports enthusiast. He watched the Redwings with his grandpa and the Detroit Tigers and Pistons with his dad.

When he was in fifth grade his family moved to a farmhouse. They had horses and hogs, sheep, goats, rabbits, chickens, and pigeons. The whole family was in 4-H, and it was a fabulously fun time for all of them. Mark, along with his brother and three sisters, had daily chores, and they showed sheep and horses at fairs.

Ten-year-old Mark was showing his pony, Penny, at the local fair. "It was for Showmanship so I had Penny in the ring on a halter and leash, like dog obedience training for horses," Mark said. "I weighed barely 70 pounds, and she dragged me around that ring like she owned me."

His dad and mom were in the bleachers nearby. His dad stood and started down the steps. Mark's mom grabbed his belt and said, "Don't you dare." She knew Mark was not in danger. The worst thing that could happen was that Penny could take off on a run. Ultimately, the worst thing would be to rob Mark of the opportunity to be independent, to conquer another obstacle. The judge must have been impressed that Mark never let go of Penny's rope – and Mark took home a blue ribbon. "For surviving," Mark jokes.

Mark commends his parents. "They had the courage to let me try whatever I wanted. They never put limitations on me. I tried everything – riding a bike, ice skating, playing baseball, football; I even drove a go kart. I always fell or crashed, always head first, and that meant lots of trips to the Emergency Room. My parents never freaked about it."

His parents instilled in him a "never quit" spirit. Mark resolved to be fiercely independent so they wouldn't have to worry about him or be ashamed of him. Mark greatly appreciates the many people who supported him – his parents and siblings, his relatives, his doctors. He is very grateful for teachers, coaches, friends and mentors. Mark commends the people who saw his potential, offered him opportunities, encouraged him and treated him the same as everyone else.

When Mark was in seventh grade, his physical education teacher asked him to be manager for the seventh grade boys' basketball team. The coach told Mark's parents, "That kid knows so much about basketball!"

Then the varsity coach asked him to be manager on game nights. At a varsity game Mark met Coach Raffin, who was announcing.

Every year Coach Raffin visited the middle school ninth grade gym classes to recruit for the track team. He recognized Mark from the varsity game so he called on Mark to help with a hurdle demonstration. Mark said, "I was tiny, and I was on my tippy toes trying my best to straddle that hurdle." Raff said to the class, "If this little guy can do it, anyone can do it. Now give the guy a round of applause!" Mark was so fired up, he signed up for high school track on the spot and recruited all his buddies to sign up too.

Mark had a passion for sports, and Coach Raff stoked the fire. For the first three weeks of track season, he had Mark practice with everyone else. As you can imagine, it was tremendously difficult for Mark, physically. He developed great respect for the efforts of athletes; he realized and appreciated how hard it is to get in shape to run competitively. Coach Raff gave Mark nice uniform warm-ups and coaching responsibilities – groups to supervise, uniforms to sort and records to keep. Mark loved going to all the big meets with the team. That was the beginning of Mark's love of track and field.

When Mark was in college, he went back to do some coaching with Raff. Early in the season Mark was complaining that the kids weren't listening. Raff said gruffly, "Find a way to get the job done, Corless!" Mark says excitedly, "That was the greatest compliment he could've ever given me! Raff never chewed on anyone like that unless he knew they could take it."

"Find a way."
That's Mark's mantra — in all things.

"Who or what hindered you?" I asked.

Mark replied, "Many things hindered me, but they didn't stop me. The biggest barriers were, and still are, put there by adults who are too willing to judge my capability based on my physical appearance."

Mark was crystal clear about his passion to coach. He saw coaching as a way to have a tremendous positive impact on kids. In college, he majored in physical education. One of his professors taught four foundational classes. Most students got A's in his classes, but not Mark. C's showed up on his report card.

Mark's professor told him, "You don't look like a coach or a physical education teacher. No one will ever hire you in this profession. You should find another major."

"He made assumptions based on my physical appearance. He didn't know what I was capable of," Mark says. "I talked to the head of the department, and that professor was no longer allowed to grade me." *Mark found a way.* And he continued to pursue a physical education major.

Over and over again throughout Mark's professional career, he faced that same obstacle when he applied for athletic director positions.

Many years later he applied for an athletic director's job in Colorado. After the job interview Mark was told, "You are by far the most qualified person for the job, but the superintendent doesn't think you look the part." People on interview boards – consistently, repeatedly, could not see beyond Mark's "unique physique."

By focusing only on his physical appearance, they missed what is truly important. They missed Mark's brilliance – his expertise, knowledge, positivity, and wisdom. They missed Mark's Spirit – his tenacity, adaptability, compassion and enthusiasm. They missed Mark's resilience.

Eventually, many people *did* see his capabilities. Mark's career culminated in the jobs of his dreams. He became the director of athletics for the 12th largest high school in Minnesota and eight years later, the activities director of an entire school district. His passion and persistence paid off!

Mark says, "I like making positive things happen for myself. I *love* helping others make positive things happen for themselves. That fires me up!"

For eleven years Mark taught emotionally impaired students. He coached simultaneously. At one point he was a teacher, coach and the middle school athletic director. Wherever he went, Mark took advantage of every opportunity to make positive things happen for kids and staff.

In teaching Mark focused on what his students could do well. He believes most are intelligent, but other issues get in the way. Mark made a point to find students' strengths, to make sure they knew he recognized their strengths and to say it often. He also got other colleagues to do the same.

One of Mark's wonderful success stories is about Missy (not her real name), a really smart student who wouldn't talk. She had been allowed to go through sixth grade without talking. When she came to Mark's class as a seventh grader, he knew she had likely been traumatized, but he wasn't about to put up with her not talking. He looked for a way . . .

Mark had an idea. He enlisted the help of the principal, other teachers and even the superintendent of schools. One day Mark and Missy were in the hallway, and the principal walked toward them. Mark looked at her and said, "Missy, what did you just say about the principal? Did you call him a jerk?" At first she looked horrified, but she got this gleam in her eye. She started saying, "Yes" or "No." Mark kept up the shtick and invited other colleagues to join in. He even accused her in front of the superintendent. By the end of the year, Missy was having full conversations. The next year as an eighth grader, she finally had friends, and one teacher had to ask Missy and her friend to be quiet! Mark used his magic – and *he found a way*.

To really see Mark, we must look at his heart, his resilient spirit. He says, "Resilience? It's how you view challenges, whatever they are. It's about *finding a way* to get beyond problems that arise and move forward, and really let the problems go; leave them behind.

Mark is clear about what it takes to be resilient. His guiding principles are:

➤ Take personal responsibility -- for your own success, failure, happiness

➤ Focus on what you can control

➤ Talk to yourself in a positive way

- ➢ Study successful people (Mark's favorites are John Wooden, Joe Newton, Eckhart Tolle, and Malcolm Gladwell)

- ➢ Focus on what you want to happen, not what you're afraid might happen

Mark is intentional about his purpose: to make a positive difference in the lives of others – every day.

Every night, he has to pass the "mirror test." He says, "I look at myself in the mirror and say, 'Did you do your best?' If the answer is, 'yes,' then I'm golden. If it isn't, I resolve to do better tomorrow."

Mark courageously, consistently and persistently *finds a way* to make a positive impact. He is most definitely "golden."

His dad says, "Mark has made us better people."

Those of us who know Mark wholeheartedly agree.

"Resilience is not overcoming, but becoming."
-Sherri Mandell

146

Points to Ponder

1. What are your gems about Mickie's, Melissa's and/or Mark's resilience?

2. When and how have you been resilient? Celebrate that!

3. In what current situation might you be more resilient? How will you do that?

Jan Glowe-Janke

Part Three

Jazz Up Your Joy with S.P.L.A.S.H. Habits

My God-given purpose for this life is to SPLASH his love and joy onto everyone. Furthermore, it is to guide you to your joy. Thank you for being here, for showing up so I can live my mission with you!

I will share six practical ways to jazz up your joy.

SPLASH is an easy acronym to remember. Each letter stands for a verb, an action you can take, a habit you can create. With each action, you are training your brain to be more positive and developing a proclivity for positivity.
The results will be . . . glorious!

Jan Glowe-Janke

Chapter 13

Smile

"A smile is the prettiest thing you can wear."
-Chuck Glowe

I can still hear my dad saying those words! I remember walking down the main street in Jonesville, Michigan, with him when I was little, and Dad would whisper, "When you smile at people, it can really brighten their day." Dad taught me to be a smiler, and I am eternally grateful. He gave me a multitude of gifts by encouraging me to wear a smile.

Smiling Abounds with Benefits

"Each time you smile you throw a little feel-good party in your brain." [15]

Doesn't that make you smile just thinking about it? I love the idea of having feel-good parties in my brain!

Smiling relieves stress. It lowers your heart rate and your blood pressure. It strengthens your immune system. Smiling makes a person look better and younger. Smiling can improve your confidence, memory, creativity, productivity, problem-solving, decision-making and longevity. Which of those benefits of smiling make you want to smile more?

A smile is contagious. You probably know that from personal experience. If you see a person smiling, you smile automatically, don't you? Or at least it probably makes you feel more joyful. There's actually scientific evidence behind that. "Neurons that fire both when we observe and when we take part in an action are called mirror neurons. When we see someone smile, mirror neurons stimulate our own smiling." [16]

Just Smile

Let's take time out for a smile right now.

1) Take a breath. Close your eyes.

2) Smile. However big or small, it doesn't matter.

3) Now hold that smile for a few breaths.

4) Take it to your heart. Really feel that smile in your face and in your body.

How did smiling make you feel? Participants I have coached in classes say that smiling causes them to feel calm, relaxed, lighter, and energized.

Let's try it another way. You will need a pencil for this. Really. Please get a pencil.

1) Put the pencil in your mouth horizontally.

2) Smile, just a little bit, feel the corners of your mouth turning up.

3) Now smile so big that it includes those muscles, those laugh lines around your eyes.

How does that make you feel?

That is called an authentic smile of happiness. It includes all the muscles in your face, your cheeks, and your eyes. It is dubbed the Duchenne smile, named for the French scientist who described and studied it.

Some research shows that even a fake smile can improve your mood and reduce stress. You've heard the phrase, "Fake it till you make it"? I like to think of it differently: "Act 'as if' until you become it."

Thoughts about Smiling

"A happy heart makes the face cheerful" (Proverbs 15:13 NIV). That proverb might lead us to think that we smile when we are joyful. But continue on to verse 30.

"A cheerful look brings joy to the heart" (Proverbs 15:30 NIV). That proverb would lead us to think that joy begins with our smile. I also wonder if the writer meant it's *our own* cheerful look or *someone else's* cheerful look that brings joy to the heart. Maybe both!

Global spiritual leader, Thich Nhat Hanh, captures the essence of both proverbs beautifully:

> *"Sometimes your joy*
> *is the source of your smile,*
> *but sometimes your smile*
> *can be the source of your joy."*

Comments about Smiling from my Splash-ees

"A smile creates openness in a relationship; it's like a welcome."

"A smile is instant energy increase!"

"Smiling is like a magnet. It pulls people toward us."

Action Steps

1. *Smile*

Smile on purpose. And *notice:* What effect does your smile have on you? What effect does your smile have on those around you?

2. *Create a Smile File*

I thank my 90-year-old friend, Con, for the fabulous idea of a smile file. In his smile file he has pictures of people he loves and fun events, special notes and cards. He goes to his smile file when he needs a "pick-me-up."

3. *Have a Smile File Party*

Gather your friends and/or family at a fun place or on a Zoom meeting. Share some goodies from your Smile File. Your Smile File Party can throw a feel-good party in your brain and heart!

4. *Stop and Smile*

Next time you feel worried, nervous, stressed, angry or anxious, just stop. Take a breath and put on a SMILE. Stay with that smile. Feel it—on your face and in your body. Notice what happens as a result of your smile.

Jan Glowe-Janke

Chapter 14

Play

"We don't stop playing because we grow old; we grow old because we stop playing."
-George Bernard Shaw

> ➢ What did you do for fun when you were a child?

> ➢ How did you play?

> ➢ What did you lose yourself in?

I asked those questions of a dozen friends, and every one of them "lit up" when they talked about their childhood play. They built tents and forts and dams. They farmed, flew jets, fought battles and piloted ships. They rode bikes, rolled down hills, walked, skipped, ran, skated, jumped rope, hula-hooped and hop-scotched. They played with Matchbox cars, marbles, G.I. Joes, action figures, dolls, building blocks, boxes, bowls, pans, Legos, Tinker Toys and balls—footballs, basketballs, softballs, whiffle balls, tether balls and splash balls. They played in the streets, in sandboxes and in rivers, woods and fields.

Most everyone said they played games with the neighborhood kids. They played tag, hide and seek, red rover, kick the can and king or queen of the mountain.

"We were outside *all the time!*" Many kids had to go home when the streetlights came on or when they heard a dad or mom's whistle. Childhood was a time to feel free, be creative and let imaginations run wild.

Jackie had a horse – pretend, of course. She galloped through the streets, jumped over shrubs and tied her horse to the porch railing when she came in for lunch.

Our grandsons had great imaginations too. Zac launched the ship which was a big white Styrofoam square; Jake climbed on board, and they paddled away into grand adventures. Those sailor boys fought off scary sea monsters and battled pirates, all within a stone's throw of our dock. They always returned home victorious and laden with treasures.

Imaginations shifted into overdrive in October. Jake's most memorable Halloween was when Zac outfitted him as an Orc, a foot soldier from *The Lord of the Rings*. Zac created elaborate armor, a shield and a sword. Jake is still in awe of that costume.

My creative friend Lindy could always be counted on to design clever costumes. One Halloween she was decked out as Little Bo Peep. She worked her Lindy-magic and turned me into her sheep!

Cherie and her buddies Butch and Phil concocted all kinds of stuff. They met at the picnic table for their planning sessions. Listen in as they "design" an underwater fort:

> "We could use my mom's old card table for a frame."

> "Yah, and then we could wrap it in old shower curtains."

> "Yah, and then we could sink it and hold it down with cement blocks."

> "Yah, and then we could cut my dad's old garden hose into three pieces and attach it to the side to breathe through."

> "Yah, and we could attach the hose to inner tubes on top of the water to keep it up in the air."

> "Yah, I'll get some duct tape and we can start."

. . . No matter that it all collapsed when they put it in the water!

Hopefully your own memories of your childhood play are coming to mind. Reminisce! Feel the delight of delving into those memories. Talk about the ways you played with your kids and grandkids and friends. And feel your energy level, your joy, rise to the roof!

In childhood, for most of us, play was a way of life. We played automatically... until the responsibilities of adulthood began to creep in and crowd out thoughts of play.

How can we bring the play, the fun, the creativity and imagination of our childhoods into our adult lives? Let's vow right now to never stop playing. We can't help growing older, but we don't have to "grow old!"

A playful *spirit* is essential to keep us youthful. Who do you know that makes everything fun?

Jack's nephews say they like to play with Uncle Jack because "he has a kid's brain." That must mean he's fun! He keeps that playful spirit alive, even though he's well into adulthood.

We went to a restaurant with a different friend named Jack and his family. While we waited for dinner, Jack started a game of "hide the cork." It was at-the-table entertainment – great fun for the little kids and the big kids!

Nanny

I have to tell you about Linda's Nanny who kept her playful spirit all the days of her life – all 106 years and 50 weeks of her life!

Nanny loved to laugh, and she loved to gather people 'round. When Nanny was in her nineties, she lived in a senior apartment building. She put a table for jigsaw puzzles at the end of the hallway. The puzzles, Nanny's home-made cookies and sounds of laughter lured lots of residents and served as a lifeline for some who had no friends or family nearby.

When Nanny was 103 she had to have two of her front teeth fixed. When they were finished, she looked in the mirror and exclaimed, "Look how good I look! I think I'll start dating!"

Linda turned to the dentist and said, "This is your fault. You're going to drive them!" (Which also shows you – the apple didn't fall too far from the Nanny tree!)

When someone asked Nanny about going to a nursing home, she said, "If they try to put me in a home, I'll run away!" Nanny got her wish. She passed peacefully in her own bed, just before her 107th birthday.

Linda and her adult children, Nick and Anna emceed Nanny's memorial service. Everyone there celebrated her love of family, her fortitude and her sense of fun. Together, we loudly, gratefully, and joyfully laughed Nanny to heaven. Afterwards, our friend Bob said, "I had more fun at that funeral than I do at some parties!"

Nanny chose to keep her playful spirit, to everyone's delight. She never grew "old."

What Is Play?

Psychiatrist Stuart Brown is the founder of the National Institute for Play. He says, "What all play has in common is that it offers a sense of engagement and pleasure, it takes the player out of a sense of time and place and the experience of doing it is more important than the outcome."[17]

Benefits of Play

"The beneficial effects of getting just a little true play can spread through our lives, actually making us more productive and happier in everything we do." [18]

Research shows that play:

> ➤ keeps us fit physically and mentally

> ➤ energizes us and enlivens us

> ➤ eases our burdens

> ➤ renews our natural sense of optimism

> ➤ fuels our imagination, creativity and problem-solving ability

> ➤ can heal emotional hurts and pain

> ➤ makes us more resilient

Your List of Play Possibilities

Think of fun times you've had, recently or not-so-recently. Think of times you've laughed and felt light-hearted, and you were so engaged you lost all track of time. What activities have you done just for fun? Celebrate the ways you already play!

As you read this chapter, consider making a list of *Play Possibilities*.

My friend Sue went on a retreat up north with three friends who love board games. They played thirty-one games in less than three full days. When not playing, they were walking, hiking, shopping, eating, sleeping and enjoying the beautiful starry sky. That sounds delightful to me! Planning a game-playing retreat with my own girlfriends is at the top of my *Play Possibilities List*.

What is your idea of fun? Play, like joy, is just not a one-size-fits-all. I love Bananagrams and playing cards, but the mere thought of inside games is pure torture for my husband. Give him a track meet and time with coaching buddies, and he's in his happy zone.

Get ready to read about people who are intentional about spending time in their "Happy Zone." They play a lot, and they play well. I'm thinking about asking them to adopt me. When I tell you all the wonderful ways they play, you may be knocking on their doors too – or better yet, you may be inspired to imitate some of the ways they play.

Are you ready to create your list of *Play Possibilities*?

Susie and Tim

They gear every day around being active. Most every morning they go for a bike ride. To cool down they play a couple games of Quixx, a dice game. Then they play ping pong.

Susie and Tim are avid pickle ball players. They meet friends and play outside. Players bring their own chairs for the sidelines, and they pile nearby picnic tables with fruit, water and snacks – that was pre-COVID. Now, in the midst of COVID, they bring buckets of Lysol spray, Wet Ones, masks and gloves. They are definitely adaptable.

Tim likes to go cherry picking in Traverse City, Michigan, with family members of all ages. Their cherry-pit spitting tournaments are everyone's favorite!

Susie is an on-the-go gal so it's no surprise that she loves yard work. Most of us say, "Yard *work*," but not Susie. Mowing and tending her flower and vegetable gardens – it's all play to her. On her birthday she got a lawn mower for a gift – and she was happy about it!

What else do they do for fun? They are geocaching fanatics! Tim describes geocaching as "A family-friendly treasure hunt using GPS technology. It's using multimillion-dollar satellites to look for treasures hidden in the woods." Just so you know, the treasures are often from the Dollar Store!

The treasures might be trinkets like flashlights, key chains or toys for the kids. Sometimes the first person to find the cache gets a bigger prize such as a $25 gas card. Often the idea is to take something and leave something. Susie and Tim love the searching as well as creating caches for others to find. They've geocached in every state between Michigan and Florida. They love to search for cache whether they are on bikes, hikes, snowmobiles or kayaks.

If that sounds like fun, you may check out the website, https://www.geocaching.com. There's even an app for that.

Vickie and Bert

Vickie and Bert have great family fun. Their house is grandkid friendly. A giant chalk board, a big bean bag chair, a game table, lots of paper, markers and colored pencils and shelves of books are great invitations to play. Vickie (Oma) loves it when the grandkids are playing the piano and making music and when they are outside, running in the yard and climbing trees.

They have fabulously fun family traditions. The New Year's Eve Talent Show delights the kids of all ages, including Grandma Kitty who is 99 ½ years old at the time of this writing. Everyone joyfully anticipates the event from one year to the next.

The New Year's Eve Talent Show includes cousins and extended family. In February Bert (Pop) begins to prime the kids, "You only have ten months until the Talent Show." And it's a topic of conversation in the summer. Their seven-year-old granddaughter asked, "Oma, I have five talents. Is that too many?" As you would expect, the kids are always front and center, shining.

Their families gather for spring break for "Commotion at the Ocean." You can just imagine all the play and fun that happen there!

"The Gourd-zilla Hunt" is yet another fun family tradition. Every fall Bert rakes leaves into a tall pile in the corner of the yard. By the end of summer it's about knee-high and 12' long. He buys gourds from the Farmers' Market and throws them on the leaf piles so the kids can run and find them. But wait, it gets better! Bert marks the gourds for 25 cents, $1 and $5. To make it fair, Bert draws different starting lines for each age. The younger the children, the closer they are to the leaf pile.

You can be sure their kids and grandkids will carry on these fun family traditions. What a lively legacy!

What Keeps Us from Playing?

Mickie signed up to play golf with ladies on Mondays. On the first Monday morning she said, "I have too many things to do today. I'm going to cancel golf."

It appears that Mickie and I have the same mindset or "programming" when it comes to play. I learned that you can play when the work is all done. The problem is -- the work is *never* all done!

Our mindsets matter.

Mickie and I must schedule our play activity and keep the commitment to ourselves. We need to keep in mind that when we play, we'll come back to our work refreshed, more creative and productive.

Pay attention to your thoughts that get in the way of your play, then experiment with ways to work around those menacing mindsets. Have you ever considered having dessert first? What if we did that with play?

What if your spouse doesn't like to play? Rebecca loves to play games; her husband does not. She tried having a game night, but that flopped. Her new tactic is to find Game Nights already happening and invite herself.

Let's identify our favorite *play possibilities* and experiment with ways to make it happen. Experiment. If it works – great! If not, we can try something different and maybe with different friends. Another strategy is to write your play activity on your calendar. What gets scheduled is more likely to get done.

Your Play List

Just in case you need more ideas for your list of *Play Possibilities*, I'll share some ideas from my Facebook friends:

Hiking, biking, horseback riding, playing with a pet,

dancing, singing, walking, talking, running, ziplining,

playing Uno, Authors, cribbage, poker, Bananagrams, or board games,

kayaking, swimming, camping, croquet,

cooking, gardening, golfing, playing an instrument

creating art and crafting of any kind – sketching, scrapbooking, needlework, woodworking

taking pictures, putting jigsaw puzzles together

bowling, fishing, hunting, jeepin'

"Having fun is not frivolous."

-Sam Horn

Play is something we do for the pure enjoyment of it. Play refreshes our bodies, minds and Spirits. It is a diversion from work and worry. According to play expert Stuart Brown, "Play is a basic human need as essential to our well-being as sleep." It is something we do to take really good care of ourselves – and it keeps us from "growing old" – so let's make play a priority!

Action Steps

1. Write your Play Lists – ways you play and ways you want to play. It might help to remember ways you loved to play when you were a kid.

2. Who is genius at play? Talk with them and get ideas for your own play. Copy their play genius.

3. Stuart Brown writes, "To benefit the most from the rejuvenating benefits of play we need to incorporate it into our everyday lives." What will you do to incorporate 5 – 10 minutes of play into each day?

4. Plan your play. Schedule a fun activity or event each month.

Jan Glowe-Janke

Chapter 15

Laugh

"Laughter is a sign of deep faith, deep hope and a sign of love."

-Tessa Bielecki

What makes you laugh? Really, please stop reading and ponder that question: What makes you laugh? Jot some of your ideas here. When you're done, I'll tell you what makes me laugh.

My Kind of Humor

Slapstick humor always tickles my funny bone. I love old Liberty Mutual Insurance commercials. Indulge me for a minute while I describe my all-time favorite Liberty Mutual commercial. We see an SUV zipping down the road with two bikes on the top. The driver arrives at home, whips into his driveway and into his garage . . . of course, the bikes get peeled off the roof of the SUV, crash through the back window and bounce wildly onto the cement.

171

Maybe you are wondering why that would be my favorite commercial. Besides being slap-stick-y, it hits pretty darn close to home. Let me explain.

My husband Charlie drives a minivan. It is great for hauling all kinds of stuff. One particular afternoon we were hauling new bar stools for our kitchen island. When we arrived at home Charlie parked in the driveway. He opened the rear lift gate of the van, and we unloaded the bar stools. We carried them in through the front door and into the kitchen which is right next to the attached garage. As I set the stools around the island, I heard Charlie driving the van into the garage. Then I heard a CRASH!

. . . He thought I had closed the rear lift gate of the van.

I hadn't!

That rear window exploded into a gazillion pieces – like rear-window confetti! Everywhere! Glittery pieces of window splattered on the driveway, on the sidewalk, in my flowers and on the garage floor. We could BE a Liberty Mutual commercial!

What would you do in that situation?

I was pretty tickled by his goof, but since he wasn't smiling, I tried to stifle my grins and giggles. That only worked for about two seconds – I laughed! Nobody was hurt. It could be fixed. I laughed out loud! In just a minute I will tell you the rest of that story.

Hopefully the story made you laugh. How did you feel just now when you were laughing?

Uplifted? Happy? Unburdened? Carefree? Lighter?

Benefits of Laughter

You do know laughing is good for you; don't you? That wisdom puts you in agreement with Mayo Clinic staff. In their online article, "Stress Relief from Laughter? It's No Joke," many benefits of laughter are listed. I will highlight three of those benefits.

Laughter:

➢ Lightens your load mentally

➢ Produces a good, relaxed feeling

➢ Makes it easier to cope with difficult situations

Would you like to have your mental load lightened?

Would you like to feel more relaxed?

What difficult situation(s) would you like to cope with more easily?

Laughter really IS the best medicine! "Dr. Jan" is prescribing laughter for you.

The Rest of the Story

Now is a good time to tell you "the rest of the story." The van that Charlie drove into our garage (with the rear gate up) was a leased van. It had to be returned the next day . . . which we did, right after we hired people to come to our house and replace the van's rear window.

He bought a beautiful new midnight blue van. When it was two weeks old, I was standing in the kitchen one morning, Charlie kissed me goodbye and went into the garage. A couple seconds later I heard him start the engine. Then CRASH! CLATTER!

He had attempted to back out of the garage. But he forgot to *open* the garage door!

We could be *two* Liberty Mutual commercials!

Thankfully, there were just minor scratches on the new van. To this day we still have a garage door that is decorated with dents and wrinkles and duct tape. We still laugh about that garage door. Well, one of us laughs louder than the other.

Instinctively we know that laughter is healthy, and we love the way we feel when we laugh. My prayer for you is that you make a point to treat yourself to laughter every day . . . for the sake of your health, your joy and for the joy of everyone around you.

Action Steps

1. Victor Borge says, "Laughter is the shortest distance between two people." Who do you want to feel close to? Connect with? Laugh with that person!

2. For more laughter and social connection – which increases happiness and good health – choose from the following action steps that strike your fancy, and enjoy laughing together.

   o Look at pictures that make you laugh.

   o Reminisce about silly/funny things people have done and laugh.

   o Make a date with someone who makes you laugh.

3. Ask your friends to tell the funniest things that ever happened to them. (When I was working on a humorous speech for Toastmasters, I intentionally asked ten friends about their funniest stories. It was the laughing-est week I have ever had!)

4. What funny tales will you tell on yourself? Please share those with your friends and with me. I'll tell on myself and my mom, and hopefully, our stories will trigger tales of your own to share. My mom was famous for telling on herself. From her example, I learned that when you do goofy things, you might as well laugh about it *and* tell others so they can laugh too.

- o Mom once wore shoes from two different pairs to a funeral. Another time, she attended the "wrong" funeral. As you might imagine, the apple didn't fall far from the tree!

- o I will joyfully tell on myself. When I got married and made macaroni and cheese for the first time, I couldn't figure out why it was white. Of course, I called Mom. She asked if I added cheese. Oops!

- o I've also fallen off an exercise bike, I eat chocolate chip cookie dough, and I rarely remember the punch line of jokes. I can laugh at myself, tell on myself and create opportunities for laughter with my friends. Everybody wins!

- o Keep a journal of funny things people say do.

5. Watch reruns of TV shows that make you laugh. Thank you to my Splash Call friends for your suggestions:

- o "Coach"
- o "Cheers"
- o "I Love Lucy"
- o "Home Improvement"
- o "The Bob Newhart Show"
- o "Big Bang Theory"
- o "Laugh In"
- o "Seinfeld"
- o "Johnny Carson"
- o "The Carol Burnett Show"

If you like slapstick, I recommend:

- o Tim Conway and Harvey Korman's skit, "The Dentist."
- o And of course, YouTube videos of Liberty Mutual commercials/London Olympics

Jan Glowe-Janke

Chapter 16

Appreciate

"A simple grateful thought turned heavenwards is the most perfect prayer."

-Doris Lessing

Judy is one the most grateful people I know. She notices a thousand things she is grateful for every day. (That may only be a *slight* exaggeration!) Imagine each grateful thought from Judy winging heavenwards to God – perfect prayers.

Judy is one of the most full-of-joy people I know. I never miss an opportunity to spend time with her. One day I dropped off a package at her house, expecting only to have time for a quick hug. But she said, "Come and sit with me for a few minutes." Of course I will.

As Judy poured me a cup of tea, she asked, "Jan, do you know what I love most about you?"

Well . . . I could hardly wait to hear what she loves about me!

"I love that you are so stable. And I love it that you are always learning and growing." As you can imagine, Judy's kind words filled me up and warmed me through and through.

One particular aspect of Judy's gratitude is extraordinary. *She speaks her gratitude out loud.*

Judy speaks loving, uplifting words of affirmation to and about everyone in her fold. Later in our conversation she was talking about driving up north with her husband Jim to see their son and grandchildren. She said, "I love that about Jim – he will drive anywhere to see our kids."

A picture of Judy belongs right beside Psalm 100:4 in the Amplified Bible: *"Be grateful and say so to Him."*

Judy *lives* that Scripture.

She is grateful and she *says so* – to God and to all her peeps. Perfect prayers!

Judy's heart is filled with gratitude, and that gratitude creates joy in her. Furthermore, her grateful, loving words splash out onto everyone in her fold and fill us with joy.

Judy's words of gratitude and affirmation created a fountain of positivity in me. Thoughts of what I love most about my husband Charlie, about my friends and my family filled me. Her words also turned my 'appreciation radar' up several notches. I became more observant about the gratitude being spoken around me.

Benefits of Feeling Gratitude and Appreciation

"God has His own little divine dopamine that allows us to feel better . . . When we focus on gratitude, when we focus on love and peace, it's as if we have our thumb pushing on that dopamine dispenser in our brains. When that dopamine floats through us . . . You get that sense of peace and it washes over you." [19] Susan Whitcomb's description captures our Creator's design. God wired us to experience a bunch of benefits when we are grateful.

In her podcast Susan Whitcomb says research shows gratitude helps us:

➢ Improve our immune system
➢ Become more creative
➢ Become more resilient
➢ Find new meaning in the difficulties of life
➢ Find new meaning from how we used to be to how the Lord is leading us to be

Family Stories about Appreciation

When I was really little, before I could read or write, I "wrote" thank you notes with my mom. I would sit on her lap, and sometimes my hand would be on hers "helping" her write the note. Other times I would hold the pen, and Mom would guide my hand. Mom was famous for her wonderful letters to family and friends. I am forever grateful for her living example of the joy and connection that writing creates.

My sister-in-law, Kim, had a rule. Her daughters had to write thank you notes before they could use, play with or wear gifts they received. I treasure those written (and spoken) words of appreciation from my nieces. Mom would applaud Kim's "rule."

Browsing in the Dollar Store is a delightful thing to do with my niece Katy and great-niece Natalie. It was especially fun to see things from Natalie's four-year-old point of view. Natalie picked up a magic wand and asked her mom if she could have it. When Katy said, "Yes," Natalie did a happy dance right there in the aisle, then hugged her mom and squealed, "Thank you! Thank you, Mom!" At Natalie's outpouring of joy and gratitude, Katy practically did her own happy dance. She said, "When you are so thankful, it makes me want to give you more!"

> *My gem: Gratitude sparks generosity and joy!*

I Appreciate and I'm Saying So

"Think with great gratitude of those who have lighted the flame within us."

-Albert Schweitzer

God has loaned so many wonderful people to me! I think with great gratitude of those who teach and encourage, those who have "lighted the flame" within me.

I appreciate Kim Avery. Her teaching and coaching as well as her example have made a huge impact on me, professionally and personally. Kim leads by serving, and she consistently encourages coaches to keep moving forward into our calling. Kim is one of the most generous and joy-filled people I know.

I appreciate Dr. Sheila Fitzgerald, my professor at Michigan State University, who enthusiastically taught that teaching English means teaching the language arts. She provided foundational philosophy and a wealth of lesson ideas to guide students into the joy of reading, writing, speaking and listening. She poured her passion into me, and it splashed through me onto my middle school English students. I am forever grateful for Sheila's inspiration and friendship.

I deeply appreciate the many friends who "get me." You know what I mean by that, don't you? Those friends who see into our hearts and bring out the best in us. This conversation with Nancy, my friend since college, is an example:

She asked, "Do you stress over writing your book?"

"Yes!"

"Do you analyze it to death?"

"Yes!"

"Do you feel like it has to be perfect?"

"Yes!"

Nancy prayed, "God, give Jan your words, let the writing flow – and give her joy in the process."

Beautiful Notes of Appreciation

I will share with you two beautifully-written notes from more friends who get me. Hopefully they will inspire you to write notes of appreciation.

Dear Jan,

Visiting you is like curling up with a great book, engaging, joyful, deeply satisfying AND – you <u>do not</u> want it to end! Thank you, my friend, for welcoming me into your home. I love sharing our worlds; you have a heart beyond measure, and I am so thankful for the time we spend together!

Love,
Sue

Jan - my sister, my friend, you have been my rock through this long journey with Wendell.

Your gifts, your prayers, your visits have meant so much to both of us. You even shared your special rock with Scripture from Claire. It's good to know whenever I need a hug you are there in a flash, not just once, but three times.

My heart sings to your heart. Know that gratitude for you fills me to capacity. Thank you!

Love,
Mary

"Feeling gratitude and not expressing it is like wrapping a present and not giving it."
-William Arthur Ward

Sue and Mary wrapped their gifts of grateful words and gave them to me. Their lovely notes are on a shelf where I see them every day. Eventually I will put them in my smile file. Hopefully they have sparked ideas for writing your own notes of appreciation.

Take Appreciation Deeper ~ Savor

Think of a friend you treasure or an experience you cherish. Close your eyes and stay in that good feeling for a few seconds; savor it.

My definition of savor is to enjoy something so much that you are compelled to pause, breathe it deeply into your heart and feel truly grateful. In his book *The Law of Happiness*, Dr. Henry Cloud writes, "Savoring is the discipline of simply focusing on and fully tasting life – feeling your feelings, noticing what is around you, celebrating the good things that are before us each and every day."

Savoring for twelve or more seconds actually weaves positivity into the fabric of our brains. [20]

My niece Karolyn is intentional about teaching her sons to savor. Each night Karolyn asks Charlie and Lucas, "What were the highlights of your day?" One night, Charlie answered, "Mom, I loved it when you played hockey with me in the driveway!" (Karolyn told me she was surprised at that because they only played for about five minutes because that was all she had.)

Kids have a knack for knowing the most important things of life – especially when it comes to play and time with people they love. Jeff, a former student, and his wife took their three kids on a bike ride then they went for ice cream. As he tucked his four-year-old into bed that night, Hayden said, "Dad, this was the best day of my life!"

"Gratitude is one of the most medicinal emotions we can feel.
It elevates our moods and fills us with joy."
-Sara Avant Stover

Think of someone or something you enjoy. Now close your eyes and stay with that sweet savoring, appreciating, blessed feeling for twelve seconds or more.

Bask in the beauty. Linger in the love. Soak it all into your soul.

Action Steps

1. Keep a gratitude journal. I highly recommend *The 90-Day Gratitude Journal* by S.J. Scott and Barrie Davenport.

2. Think about someone you are grateful for. Acknowledge a specific strength or value and the impact on you. Ask that person, "Do you know what I love about you?" Then speak your appreciation. *Say so* to that person.
And say "Thank you!" to God.

3. Send *a handwritten note* to a person you appreciate.

4. Appreciate something about a person who is difficult for you. SAY SO to that person and/or write a note to *say so*.

5. Write a list of people, sights, sounds, smells and activities you appreciate. I'll share some of my delights; you are welcome to "borrow" or add your own: Hugs, smiles, talking and laughing with friends, the yummy smell of warm chocolate chip cookies, reading a good book, glorious sunsets.

Jan Glowe-Janke

Chapter 17

Speak Life

"Pleasant words are a honeycomb, sweet to the soul and healing to the bones."

Proverbs 16:24 NIV

Speak Life ~ It Is Essential to Your Well-Being and Your Joy

Did you see the movie, "A League of Their Own?" It's a 1992 film about the All-American Girls Professional Baseball League during World War II. Tom Hanks plays the coach, Jimmy Dugan. Coach's famous words still ring in my ears:

"Are you crying? Are you crying? ARE YOU CRYING? There's no crying! There's no crying in baseball!"

(You have to see and hear it for yourself to really appreciate it.)

There is no crying in baseball, and

there is no negativity in creating your spirit of joy!

No complaining, no blaming, no judging, no gossip,

no criticism --

of yourself or others or situations. Choose to speak life!

> *Speak life to yourself.*
> *Speak life to others.*
> *Speak life into your situations.*

"The tongue has the power of life and death."
Proverbs 18:21a NIV

The words we speak tremendously impact our emotions and our energy.

You are welcome to experiment with this idea. Begin to notice your emotions when you *think* certain words and phrases. Also pay attention to your emotions when you *hear* certain words and phrases. Observe the words that boost your joy and energy. Notice the words that zap your energy, your Spirit.

Here is a good starting place – because it happens often. When you first see a friend or even an acquaintance, and that person asks, "How are you?" What is your response?

Responses I have heard recently are, "Getting by." "Okay." "Can't complain."

On the other hand, we have people like Allen and Amzie. Every single time I see Allen, I purposely ask how he is because his answer is predictable and delightful. He always says:,"I am blessed!" He says it enthusiastically, emphatically and with a smile – no matter what trials he is going through.

Amzie takes it a step further. His response to "How are you?" is, "I am blessed and highly-favored!" It is immediate and like Allen's, and it is always enthusiastic. Both gentlemen intentionally choose to speak life.

And there's Todd who will predictably reply, "Walking on sunshine!" or "Living the dream!"

We can follow their lively examples. How will you respond the next time someone asks, "How are you?"

Speak Life to Yourself

"The brain believes what you tell it most. And what you tell it about you it will create," writes Shad Helmstetter, author of *What to Say When You Talk to Yourself*. That's one reason it is essential to speak life to yourself.

Self-criticism is a habitual way of thinking for many of us. I know because I hear it in conversations with friends and coaching clients. I also hear that voice in my own head. It is the voice of fear. It limits our options. It inhibits our opportunity to make good choices. It gets in the way of having a brand new adventure.

Many of us tend to second guess ourselves or beat ourselves up with thoughts like, "That was a dumb thing to say," "I'm not good enough," or "They'll think I'm crazy."

The thoughts we think about ourselves and the words we say to ourselves tremendously impact our emotions and our behavior. That bears repeating and imprinting on our hearts:

The words we speak tremendously impact our emotions and our behavior.

What *do* you say when you talk to yourself?

Maybe you've said to yourself, "I'm so tired," or "I'm such a procrastinator," or "I'm so bad at remembering names."

I plead guilty. If you do too, then we both need to make a conscious effort to stop criticizing ourselves. Let's stop those negative words. You know the ones I mean; they are the ones that crush our spirits, zap our energy and steal our joy.

We do have the power to tell our brains what we want it to create! Let's speak life to ourselves – to expand our options, increase our opportunities and open us up to new adventures.

A 3-Step Process to Speak Life to Yourself

If you want to speak life, consider practicing the following 3-step process:

1. BECOME AWARE of what you are thinking and saying to yourself.

2. STOP all life-draining words. (Criticism, blame, complaint, judgment, gossip, worry)

3. REPLACE them with words of life.

Awareness is the first step. What you are aware of, you can change. Notice your thoughts and your words. When you notice your thoughts and your words of life, celebrate that, even with a little fist pump or a "Yay you!" And keep speaking those words of life.

When you hear yourself speaking negatively, *Stop!* Say out loud, "Cancel! Cancel!"

Replace the negativity with words of life:

> ➤ I am kind.

> ➤ I am loved.

> ➤ I am joyful.

> ➤ I am calm.

> ➤ I am healthy.

> ➤ I am courageous.

> ➤ I am light and lively.

Two Powerful Words

"Whatever you attach consistently to the words 'I am,'
you will become."

-Zig Ziglar

The question that begs to be asked is: What do you want to become?

Let's make a conscious effort to shift from life-draining words to life-giving words. Here's an example: It was a gray, rainy day, and I was feeling tired and draggy. I curled up on the couch.

1. *Awareness*: I caught myself thinking, "I don't have any energy. I don't feel like doing anything." My negative words sent up red flags.

2. *Stop*: Aloud I said, "Cancel! Cancel!"

3. *Replace*: I shifted my thinking. I said to myself, "I am happy! I am healthy! I am active, and I feel terrific!" I borrowed the lively words of success legend, W. Clement Stone, who began every day by exclaiming, "I feel happy! I feel healthy! I feel terrific!"

I stood up, put on a smile and proclaimed, "I am happy! I am healthy! And I feel terrific!"

Those words energized me – enough to get me out the door for a walk.

Does that sound a little corny or contrived to you? Part of me was reluctant at first too.

Ponder the profound impact
of my thoughts and words
on my emotions and on my behavior.

Tired, no-energy thoughts caused me to plop on the couch. Happy, healthy thoughts and words motivated me to move. Making the shift to speaking words of life works every time – every time I remember to do it. The positive results of speaking life make me a believer.

I chose to declare what I wanted to become: "I am active!" I made a proclamation. Maybe you prefer the word declaration or affirmation. You may read the dictionary definitions below and choose which one suits you and your situation.

Declaration – Affirmation – Proclamation

According to the Merriam Webster Dictionary:

A declaration is an announcement.

An affirmation is a positive assertion; a validation

A proclamation is a public declaration, typically insistently, proudly or defiantly and in either speech or writing.

Whatever you name it, remember to use the words, "I am . . ." and follow it with what you want to become. It is a powerful way to speak life to yourself.

Think about what you want to become. Obviously you want to be joyful. What will it take to get to your joy? Let's review the sections you have already read. Some possible declarations are:

- ➤ I smile easily.
- ➤ I have a playful spirit.
- ➤ I laugh easily.
- ➤ I appreciate my energy.
- ➤ I enthusiastically speak life to myself and to everyone around me.
- ➤ I am purpose driven.
- ➤ I am strong – physically, spiritually and emotionally.

"Learning to build the best in yourself—by learning to give yourself a refreshing new program of self-speak— is one of the greatest gifts you will ever give to yourself."

--Shad Helmstetter

Give Your Self-Talk Extra Power

Smile! A smile gives your words more energy.

For even more energy, *stand up!*

For over-the-top energy, *stand like a superhero* as you speak. You know that pose – Arms raised in the air, feet hip-distance apart – like your favorite superhero. Imagine your cape streaming out behind you! Social psychologist Amy Cuddy calls that stance a "power pose." I encourage you to watch her inspiring TED Talk, *Your Body Language May Shape Who You Are.*

Speak Life into Others

"If you don't have something nice to say, don't say anything at all!" Did you hear those words from your mom too?

When my friend Chris says, "Lord, keep one hand on my shoulder and the other one over my mouth," it always makes me laugh. But really, it is a profound prayer.

I am responsible for the words that come out of my mouth; you are responsible for the words that come out of your mouth. That means we must "bite our tongues" and consciously choose *not* to speak words that hurt, discourage or destroy. I have *never* been sorry when I have held my tongue. But many times I have spoken words I want to take back, words I regret. If you too have known the heartache of speaking words that hurt others, usually people you love most, and you desire to be intentional about speaking life – you are welcome to join me in Chris' prayer.

> *"Lord, please keep one hand on my shoulder and the other hand over my mouth."*

How about when you *think* something nice? Say it out loud, of course. Everyone around you will be lifted up by your pleasant words. Speak life to your spouse, children, grandchildren, friends, family, co-workers, church members, to the people who serve you. Some examples are: "You give the best hugs," "Your smile brightens my day," and "You are such a good helper."

Who Speaks Life into You?

What life-giving words have others spoken to you? Pause. Let your heart remember, and let those words warm your heart again. I'll share some of my gems in hopes they will help you recall pleasant word-treasures.

On my tenth birthday card, my great-grandma wrote, "I love you more than tongue can tell, Janet." My mom once said to me, "I love that you are kind to older people." And Delores wrote, "I am so proud to be your colleague."

The life-giving words of others are heart-warming, long-lasting gifts. We can appreciate and savor those sweet words. We can also use them as examples of how to speak life into others.

> *It is essential to speak life to ourselves*
> *and to others.*
> *Our words have a powerful impact*
> *on our emotions, our energy and our behavior.*

Speak Life into Your Situations

In addition to speaking life to myself, and more specifically to my body to get it moving, I have to make a conscious effort to speak life into situations – especially situations that require neatness and efficiency. I tend to get many projects going simultaneously which means I often accumulate piles – mainly in my home office and on the island in my kitchen. A couple years ago I had reached a perilous point. I was drowning in piles of scrappy notes, books and projects. I couldn't find the things I wanted and needed; I was overwhelmed and frustrated.

What causes you to feel overwhelmed or frustrated?

How do we speak life in those situations?

I began by saying, "I am organized." "I can easily find everything I want and need." Those statements were *far* from the truth, but I forced myself to say them – and to say them with a smile. I know that when I change my energy, by smiling, then I change my situation, my emotions and my behavior.

Instead of focusing on the problem, I decided to focus on what I wanted.

Whatever we focus on, expands.

I wrote, "I am organized and efficient" on sticky notes and put them on my desk, on my printer, on my laptop. I continued to speak those words of life out loud. Then an amazing thing happened. After four days of speaking life to myself, my friend Allison called. She said, "My mom and I are becoming organizing coaches; can we practice on you?"

> *"See, the former things have taken place,*
> *and new things I declare;*
> *before they spring into being,*
> *I announce them to you."*
>
> Isaiah 42:9 NIV

My former things were feeling tired and drowning in piles.

The new things I declared were, "I am organized!" and "I am happy, healthy, and I feel terrific!"

I announced the new things, and they sprang into being. Well, maybe the new things didn't quite *spring* into being. Improvement is a process. The important thing is forward movement.

Speak God's Word

Another foundational aspect of speaking life is to speak the words God has given us in Scripture. What happens when we speak the word of God?

> *"Bless the Lord, you His angels,*
> *who excel in strength, who do His word,*
> *heeding the voice of His word."*
>
> Psalm 103:20 NKJV

"Give voice to God's word and see His angels respond. His angels are activated when you speak His Word!" writes evangelist Joseph Prince.

Isn't it incredible to think that we can *do something* that actually activates God's angels? All we have to do to set angels in motion is give voice to God's word. The following sentences are taken right from Scripture. Please consider speaking God's word aloud. Continually.

- ➢ "I am a child of God." (1 John 3:1)
- ➢ "I can do everything through him who gives me strength." (Philippians 4:13)
- ➢ "God has given me a spirit of power, of love and of self-control." (2 Timothy 1:7)

➢ "I am more than a conqueror." (Romans 8:37)
➢ "In all things God works for the good of those who love him." (Romans 8:28)
➢ "I am an ambassador for Christ."
   (2 Corinthians 5:20)
➢ "My body is a temple of the holy spirit."
   (1 Corinthians 6:19)
➢ "God's spirit lives in me." (1 Corinthians 3:16)
➢ "God is with me, he is mighty to save. He takes great delight in me, he quiets me with his love, he rejoices over me with singing." (Zephaniah 3:17)

If you just read those words from Scripture aloud, you have not only spoken life, you have activated God's angels!

May the words of our mouths
and the meditations of our hearts
be pleasing in your sight,
Oh Lord, our Rock and our Redeemer.
                                            Psalm 19:14 NIV

Action Steps

1. Find a declaration that resonates with you.

   Write it on sticky notes and post it by your bed, on your bathroom mirror, on the dashboard of your car. Say it out loud. Declare it every morning when you wake up and every night before you go to sleep. The more you give voice to your declaration, the better.

2. Notice energy-draining words you think or speak. Write those words on an index card. With a big dark marker, draw XXXXXXXs over those words. Cancel, cancel them. Delete those life-draining words from your vocabulary.

3. Practice the 3-step process for shifting from life-draining to life-giving words.

   o In your self-talk

   o In speaking about others

   o In speaking about a situation

4. Choose a favorite Scripture that speaks to your soul. Write it down. Say it out loud often. Visualize the angels you have set in motion.

5. Choose a person each day or each week, and intentionally speak life into that person.

Chapter 18

Hold Your Purpose in Your Heart

"Let everyone be devoted to fulfill the work God has given them to do . . . and their joy will be in doing what's right and being themselves, and not in being affirmed by others."

Galatians 6:4 TPT

Purpose. Mission. It's the work God has given you to do. It's your task, your assignment for life on this earth. And it's the foundation for true joy, the joy of knowing who you are and becoming who you are created to be.

Having a strong sense of purpose doesn't necessarily mean your life will be *easy*, but with your purpose in your heart, you'll know a peaceful joy – The joy of knowing your life matters and knowing you are making a difference. Living with your purpose in your heart frees you to live a meaningful, fulfilling life!

In this chapter you will meet people who are dear to me; I am delighted to share them with you! Enjoy these snippets and stories. See and savor the plethora of positive effects of living with passion and purpose – on each individual, on others, in the community, and in the world.

Jeanette

God put Jeanette on this earth to empower others to thrive. (You met her at the end of the Stay C.A.L.M. chapter.) When you read the following story, in her words, you will see how Jeanette empowered her young adult daughter to thrive.

"I was talking with my daughter Mackenzie after her first week of living on Mackinac Island. She said she hadn't been feeling well the last couple days and she knew it was because she had not been eating enough. Food was very expensive on the island, even at the non-tourist grocery store. To my "mama ears," this definitely hit a sour note on my piano. I could feel the urge to drive four hours north to take food to my "baby girl" or at least deposit a bunch of money in her account and rescue her from this situation.

However, the logical side of my brain prevailed so I did what I have been doing with my kids for years. First, I empathized. Next, I sent her the "you can do this/I believe in you" message by asking what she was going to do about her situation. Then I stopped talking and listened . . . for a long time . . . to let her process.

Once in a while, after much listening, I may ask my kids if they would like a suggestion, but I try to not do that too often. In this instance, I knew Mackenzie was going to be living in tourist areas for many years to come, and these types of expenses would be a reality she would need to learn to negotiate.

The good news is that Mackenzie ended up having a day off about three days later, and she was able to catch a ride to a Wal-Mart about forty minutes away to buy healthier, fresh, and much less expensive food.

Now she's learned that she has to use her days off to journey off the island and catch a ride somehow to shop for herself. She is also learning that as cool as it is to live and work on Mackinac Island, the expense is close to outweighing her income, and this will result in falling short of having enough money to pay for her college tuition in the fall.

It is hard to see her learn this lesson, but life is a much better teacher than I am, and she is more willing to listen to "life" than Mom. Just the same, I would rather have Mackenzie learn to think through these realities now, while the price tag is rather small, than in the future when she has taken on a mortgage or moved half-way around the world, only to discover she really cannot afford it.

Also, if/when needed, I can always step in this year and help make up Mackenzie's financial deficit, but I have learned over the years to not be too quick to act. My kids have amazed me time and again with their creativity and resiliency when coming up with solutions to their problems.

Plus, when they work through a solution, their character grows and so does their self-esteem, and this is so much better than just having mom or dad bail them out.

I wish I could take credit for all these parenting techniques, but the truth is that I am a certified Love and Logic instructor, so I used this professionally. However, I am also a highly satisfied customer as I believe in the Love and Logic approach to parenting. I have benefited greatly from practicing what I preached."

https://www.loveandlogic.com/

Shannon

Shannon's mission is to connect others to joyful experiences. She writes, "If I'm struggling with a decision, I go back to my mission statement, and it always steers me in the right direction. The best part about having a mission statement is that it has given me wings to try new things. For instance, I now host a weekly professional trivia show. It aligns perfectly with my mission statement, and I absolutely love it!"

Millie and Bob

Millie had an idea, a yearning. She said, "It was something God placed in my heart, and it wouldn't go away."

Millie and her husband Bob (not their real names), were approaching their mid-century mark of age; they had two grown children. Bob and Millie agreed they would have no more children. But now, here they were, nearing 50, and *Millie had a yearning, a deep yearning, in her heart. She wanted to adopt a child.*

One day Millie was in her counseling office when a parent came in to register her daughter for high school classes. Toddling behind the mom was her three-year-old daughter, a beautiful little girl from China. Millie's heart melted. That mom gave Millie a book, *The Waiting Child* by Cindy Champnella. Millie said, "Once I knew about the thousands of healthy baby girls in China who needed a home, I couldn't pretend I didn't know."

Millie admits she had a bad case of the "what-ifs?" "What if I'm too old to be a mom?" "What if this is just my desire and not God's will?" In addition to her doubts, she faced another difficult reality – Bob was still not on the same page. He continued to push-back, for a long time. And the yearning in Millie's heart wouldn't go away.

Millie prayed. She knew that Bob's heart could only be changed by God. She didn't beg or nag or plead. Many months went by. Millie had not mentioned the idea of adoption once. Bob noticed, really noticed. He mentioned to his men's accountability group that he was nearing retirement, and adoption wasn't on his radar. One friend blurted out, "It's not about you!"

It was immediately revealed to Bob these were not just words from a friend but the holy spirit speaking through his friend. His heart was changed in an instant. From then on, Bob and Millie pursued the path the Lord had laid on Millie's heart. Bob says, "When the Lord gives us a clear message of a directional change from what we originally wanted (or did not want), he *always* gives us a spirit of joyous acceptance."

As it turned out Millie and Bob filed adoption papers – on the same day their waiting child was born. Millie retired in June, turned fifty in December, and one week later she and Bob were in China holding their baby daughter in their arms.

There is one more significant thing for you to know. Bob's mom had prayed for years that one of her children would be a missionary to China. Her prayers were still working, years after she had gone home to heaven. Millie's courage to act on her passion was the answer to Bob's mother's prayer.

Becky

Becky is a bundle of energy. She's all about compassion and vitality. In coaching sessions, she often asked, "Am I doing enough? Am I enough?" She compared herself to others who did more or "bigger" things.

Becky poured herself into discovering her purpose. *Her mission is to nurture with compassion and vitality.* That sense of purpose helps her realize she is worthy of love; it has opened her eyes to see that she needs and wants to nurture herself first. She's even giving herself permission to "do nothing," to relax! A friend noticed the change in Becky; she said, "You're still robust, but you're calm!"

Becky says, "It's comforting to know I'm on the right path. It's propelling me to trust God more." Becky has taken responsibility for her joy. She speaks positively to herself. She is making decisions and acting on them instead of second guessing and comparing herself to others. She is proclaiming her purpose and celebrating the way God made her!

Dan

Dan has traveled worldwide to learn to be the best in his profession. He works incredibly hard, and he strives for perfection. Often that wears him out. After completing a project, he is exhausted and has to sleep.

Dan discovered his mission is to inspire excellence. It is *not* "*be* perfect." Knowing what he is put on earth to do helps him let go of what he is *not* to do. Dan says knowing his mission reminds him of what gives him energy, and it helps guide his decisions.

Kathy

The pain from her past was a dark cloud that weighed her down. Kathy felt trapped. She was especially burdened by her mom's criticism and negativity. Kathy was also weighed down with grief over the death of a child.

We discovered that *God put Kathy on this earth to lead others into freedom.* As she took steps to lead *herself* into freedom, she felt a huge release. She became accepting of people and things she couldn't change. She let go of others' expectations and set healthy boundaries. She shed negativity, and she lost weight. Her confidence and joy increased as she taught others better eating habits. Kathy gave herself permission to do things that made her feel alive. She's happy in her kitchen, canning and experimenting. She has canned homemade caramel, pineapple zucchini, and she's teaching her grandchildren as they help can peaches and tomatoes.

In reflecting, Kathy said, "It is such heavy baggage. I realized I was at a crossroad, and I had a choice. By accepting my grief and talking about it in coaching sessions, I found a way to set the baggage down and move on."

Kathy's mission statement is a firm foundation that empowers her to make the choice to take good care of herself and create a life she enjoys.

Janet

God put Janet on this earth to inspire life-giving faith. She led a weekly Bible study at her mother's retirement home. Janet has adapted in this time of pandemic and isolation; she cheers on the residents with letters, encouraging Scriptures and stories. Janet is intentional about speaking words of love, validation and kindness. She writes, "I used to long to do something great for many people, but now I am very happy just sowing simple seeds of lovingkindness, one person at a time." Her painting, photography and poetry point people to God's artistry. She has a heart for prayer. Her profound prayers and beautiful singing voice inspire faith.

She used to think that just because she thought of great ideas, she should be the one to do them all. Janet writes, "Discovering my mission statement and understanding who God created me to be has freed me from the dreadful burden of false guilt. False guilt is wrong thinking that comes from comparison, insecurity and fear. These realizations allow me to give myself permission to paint and write and enjoy it even though my house isn't perfectly neat and clean."

TJ

TJ is off-the-charts passionate! He is a health-centered dentist/coach; his passion for helping others through dentistry rocks him out of bed by 5 a.m. every week day. He reads, prays and studies; he practices dentistry; he coaches his patients and mentors other dentists; he teaches, encourages and inspires. He is truly one of the most energetic, enthusiastic people I have ever met.

He is incredibly focused. TJ studies, journals and reflects, and he diligently applies what he studies. While many of us are reading "wide," Facebook scrolling, for example, TJ is studying deep. Rather than reading a dozen books, he reads a few, repeatedly. He studies the works of Napoleon Hill, Bob Proctor, and his mentor, Dr. Mike Schuster.

TJ has been my weekly study partner on the phone for a decade. I am excited to introduce him to you and to share his story. Please pay attention to TJ's path as he has pursued his passion. You'll notice the "rough waters" he has navigated. You'll see people who encouraged and supported him, you'll hear profound clarifying questions, and you'll celebrate his accomplishments and joys.

TJ's mom was a nurse. As a lad he loved accompanying her on home visits. He watched his mom as she changed bandages, gave shots and talked with patients. TJ borrowed models from his mom, models of the eyeball, the hand, and the heart, and he took them to school for "show and tell." He watched television shows like "Marcus Welby," "Dr. Kildare" and "Ben Casey."

In high school, TJ was president of the Medical Explorers Club, and he worked in a hospital. He especially loved interactions and in-depth conversations with patients.

You have probably guessed it – TJ's dream was to be a doctor.

Between his junior and senior years in college he took the MCAT and applied to medical school. Then he waited. And he waited. Finally, in the spring just before graduation, he got the news. He did not get accepted. In his words, "Tragedy struck." He was devastated. "Now what?" he wondered. After much soul-searching he knew he had to "stick with it." TJ took the MCAT again and reapplied to medical school.

TJ said, "It was the first time I experienced failure."

His good friend, Father Hauser, took TJ out to dinner. He asked, "TJ, what are you going to do? How are you feeling about it?" Father Hauser helped TJ think and feel out loud, to become aware of his emotions and desires. That conversation helped TJ come up with a plan to start graduate school.

In his first semester, TJ signed up for only six credit hours. His dream of being a doctor was on hold, at best. He felt lost, and he felt like a failure.

Also, in that first semester TJ recalls sitting on a bench in front of St. Johns' Church. He could see the medical school in the distance. He was yearning, desperately hoping he would be there one day. TJ prayed, "God, what do you want me to do with my life?"

TJ drew closer to God. He had always been in relationship with God, but now he tapped even more into that infinite power. And grace. He felt as though he didn't have anything else.

In his first year of graduate school, TJ worked for an anesthesiologist. He asked TJ, "Do you ever think about being a dentist?" That was a profound question which became a turning point for TJ. Consequently, he applied to dental school, he prayed, and he asked God to show him the way.

In his second year of graduate school, TJ was tending bar one night when a group of gals walked in. One was wearing a badge that said, "Kiss me, it's my birthday." So he did. "That kiss was the beginning," TJ says. "This was the girl I'd been looking for my whole life! I felt like a GI going off to war – I didn't want to let her get away." They started dating and after eight months, they were engaged.

Fast forward to present day: TJ and Lou Ann recently celebrated their fortieth anniversary. TJ said, "I am blessed beyond belief! What we have accomplished and overcome as a couple is amazing. I reflect on all that and still feel the electricity of that first kiss."

TJ was accepted to dental school. At the same time he was number thirteen on the waiting list for medical school. He decided to go with the "sure thing." After four years of intense lectures, labs and work, TJ graduated from dental school and bought an existing dental practice. It took only three years for TJ to dislike dentistry. He wasn't happy doing "procedures." Paying attention to your passion is essential; it is also essential to pay attention to what you do not like.

Another turning point for TJ came through an invitation to hear Dr. Schuster speak; TJ seized the opportunity. He says, Dr. Schuster taught how to be a physician of the mouth, a different way to practice dentistry. In Dr. Schuster's paradigm, dentistry is about creating health instead of merely treating disease. "It was exactly what I was looking for!"

Yet another turning point for TJ came from his mom. She gave him her teeth in a Christmas stocking! She gave him "the gift" because she thought the gold had value. But the ultimate value was in the question it prompted TJ to ask: "How could you lose your teeth? You went to the dentist every six months!" It affirmed everything Dr.

Schuster was teaching: Dental health requires a comprehensive approach.

TJ is all about creating health – not treating disease. He is not a traditional dentist, not a tooth carpenter. He helps patients understand the cause of disease, and he has a proven structure to help them get beyond it. For the most part, plaque is the cause of tooth decay and gum disease. He and his team coach patients how to effectively remove plaque. His patients have the freedom to choose and participate in their excellent oral health.

TJ's top priority is to take really good care of his patients. His dentistry is his ministry. To say that he loves his work is probably the understatement of the century! To learn more, you may visit his website: http://www.drtjbolt.com

TJ participated in my Workshop, What on Earth Am I Here For? He discovered that *God put him on this earth to be a paradigm pioneer.* He says, "That purpose statement was a permission slip that gave me the freedom to be who I was all along. Knowing my purpose is vitally important for my business, my self-esteem and my family."

He holds that purpose in his heart! And he intentionally aligns his life, daily and diligently, with his purpose. The result is great focus and fulfillment for TJ and more energy and better health for the people around him.

I will share a bit more about TJ's purpose journey because there are more gems you may want to apply in your own life.

Out of TJ's purpose, his vision for his dental practice became very clear. He wanted a new building in a natural, beautiful setting where his patients could feel relaxed and comfortable. For four years, TJ envisioned it and "emotionalized" it. He dreamed. He imagined every detail about his new building, he wrote about his vision, he gained clarity and re-wrote. He spent time thinking and acting and feeling like the new building already existed. He could picture it clearly. He could feel the joy and excitement of practicing in his new office long before it ever came to fruition. He also had a strong belief that the tranquil, calming place for his practice would come about at the right time.

He hired a business coach to guide him.

TJ's long-time patient, Mike, came on board with his dream. That's what happens when you have a powerful purpose/mission and vision -- it becomes a magnet that draws people and resources to you.

TJ and Mike kept looking for property, but doors kept shutting. Finally, when they were about to give up, TJ's realtor found a pad of dirt in a wooded area in the middle of suburbia for sale. It was the sanctuary TJ had envisioned!

Was it scary for TJ? Yes! He knew not all of his patients would follow him to the new place.

Also, he had been in debt for a long time. But with encouragement from his coach and with financial help from Mike, TJ kept moving forward. He continued to hold his purpose in his heart.

It took 20 years for TJ to become an "overnight success." Now in his sixties, TJ says, "I wasn't always where I'm at." Other dentists may look at him and think it looks easy. However, it took years of following his passion. It took years of hard work and study, years of persevering through struggles and disappointments. Every step of the way, TJ intentionally practiced faith and gratitude.

TJ has persistently held his purpose in his heart. It has been his North Star. You can see how his purpose has guided his decision making. It helped him break through the terror barrier. His passion and his purpose have given him confidence and courage to live a meaningful life.

Sheri

A beautiful thing happens as you move in the direction of your passion . . . Lily pads pop up! When Sheri says "lily pads" she is referring to people, ideas and opportunities that popped up each time she took a step in line with her passion.

Our neighbor Sheri had been a distance runner in high school. It was before girls' sports were the norm, so she joined the boys' cross-country team. Sheri says, "It was the first time I realized that a person's goals may overstep the customs of the time."

When she was 48 years old, she started to run again as a way to cope with grief over the death of two dear friends. A younger co-worker was training for the Detroit Half-Marathon, and Sheri joined her in training. All the feelings and strength of being a distance runner came back! After accomplishing the half-marathon Sheri had the desire to run the Detroit Marathon the next year. And so began her 22-week training. A friend returned on his one-year leave of absence from the Marines, and they trained together. Sheri told him she wanted to try to qualify for the Boston Marathon. At first, he laughed heartily! She was silent. When he realized she was serious, he balked, "That's a very lofty goal." Silence. "Then we have to take this training to the next level," he said. And they did.

Race day arrived. Qualifying time for her age group was four hours. She made it in 3:59.19!

Then she read in *Runners' World* magazine that Boston was part of the five World Marathon Majors (WMM). Sheri ran three American WMM: Boston, Chicago and New York City. Two years later she ran marathons in London and Berlin. Done! She had accomplished her lofty goal of all five WMM . . . Then Tokyo was added! She felt deflated. No way could she save the money so quickly. But . . . Sheri's Clarklake Community rallied behind her and raised the money needed to cover the costs of her trip to Tokyo. In 2013 Sheri became the first American female to complete the six WMM. At that time only four women and six men had completed the six WMM!

Sheri writes, "Albeit, the six WMM only cover three continents . . . Hence, the phrase, 'One finish line leads to the next start line.' My friend Cindy and I continue running marathons around the globe: Cape Town, South

Africa 56K, Rio de Janeiro, New Zealand, and the pinnacle race, Antarctica, to achieve the goal of completing the Seven Continents Club. Ta-da!"

Ta-da is right!

Sheri said, "Each time I stepped, another lily pad showed up! My path became so clear."

Sheri's mission is to engage others in the flow of seeking and achieving their lofty goals.

She founded the Sole2Soul Running Club, and she has trained fifth graders, called Jr. Sole2Soul, to run a five-kilometer race. Sheri is an excellent example of one who pursues her passion – which makes life delightful and fulfilling for herself, her community, and the world.

Charlie

"God put me on this earth to coach." Those exact words came right out of my husband's mouth. If you know Charlie, you know that's not his typical kind of comment. But I tell you with an overflowing heart – it is the true-est statement ever. For the past 40+ years, I have watched him live passionately and purpose-fully. And I have witnessed his profound, far-reaching, long-lasting impact.

When Charlie retired after 45 years of coaching, I decided to make a scrapbook for him. I sent letters to his former athletes, their parents and fellow coaches requesting their thoughts and memories. I am honored to share their words with you. They testify that Charlie lives and breathes his calling to coach.

Jimmy: "Coach Janke trained us to always act like champions, when we lost, but even more so when we won. He demanded humility, discipline, goal setting and self-appraisal. But most of all he taught self-worth. He is the reason I coach. He is the reason I teach. If I can save one kid the way he saved me, well, then my life has had a purpose. Cross and track became my life and Coach Janke became my role model. He was the father so many of us didn't have."

Mark: "You are one of the greatest coaches around. I have always appreciated how organized and knowledgeable you are and how you never stop learning. On top of that, I thought it was great that you wanted us to know why we trained the way we did and how it impacted our bodies, the biology and physiology behind it. You were and still are a great role model for doing the best you can in whatever you do and every facet of your program shows it.

The most important thing I ever learned from you is the role of discipline in life. Just as Paul told Timothy to train yourself to be godly, I have concluded that I need to train and discipline myself to be godly. I have set up a training program! It's a foundation I learned from you and am now passing it on to my runners."

Sarah: "The lessons and principles I learned from Mr. Janke still guide me to this day and have shaped my life. The values of determination, goal-setting and discipline which were so much a part of our cross country philosophy also carried me through college, medical school, residency and my Navy career. The sheer joy of running and competition is still a major part of my life and has been over the last 18 years. When going through a tough experience such as a marathon or a long night on call at the hospital, I sometimes will repeat one of Mr. Janke's phrases, 'The mind controls the body.'

Mr. Janke set standards of excellence that taught us to not be satisfied with the status quo, but to always reach for the next level. Without realizing it at the time, I now see that Mr. Janke was helping to build the confidence and perseverance I needed to succeed not only in cross country, but more importantly, in life. Over the four years he was my coach, I never realized that his wisdom would so profoundly affect me. He is by far, one of the most influential people in my life."

Corey: "Before I participated in track and field at JHS I thought the only thing you had to do was show up and run fast. You taught me about conditioning, performance strategy, mental toughness and conditioning again and again."

Josh: "He pushed me hard and emphasized the importance of dedication. 'There are no short-cuts in long distance running!!!' He pointed out some of my strengths, which boosted my confidence substantially at that young age. The physical shape that I achieved under his guidance helped me accomplish my mission in Iraq, even though I graduated from JHS six years ago."

Sheri: "Your belief in me and the encouragement to do my BEST, the challenges to strive for more and the nudge to go outside my comfort zone have been so formative in the person I have become. I am blessed with two amazing sons whom I get to pass that encouragement and lessons down to. Thank you for doing more than your job and for setting a standard of expectation that helped us rise above our beliefs in ourselves."

Beth Ann: "I am so thankful I had you as a coach. I appreciate all the strategies you taught me from straight-lining to negative splitting which translate to life as well. I couldn't have asked for a better cross country, track or life coach."

Aretha: "You were disciplined, direct and intimidating, but I quickly recognized that beneath that surface you were honest, kind and appreciated that as our coach you had a responsibility to make sure that we not only improved our times but also learned important life lessons about perseverance and goal setting that would serve us well beyond high school.

Although I was (and remain) the quintessential nerd, my track, winter track and cross country experiences, along with the camaraderie and friendships of those seasons have helped define who I am, and the mother that I am, in ways much more powerful than books, experiments and algorithms. Thank you for making an indelible impression on my life."

Lezlie: "My favorite quote from Coach Janke is, 'The single greatest factor about learning how to be a self-champion in athletics is that you will have also earned to be a self-champion in life.' I have always kept the self-champion lifestyle in my mind wherever I go. I hope that someday I can carry that philosophy into my coaching with as much fervor and skill as Coach Charles Janke."

Herb: "I met Coach Janke 31 years ago at a six-day summer cross country camp at MSU. He helped start a fire under me for the sport that has shaped my life and continues to influence me. It may seem peculiar that a six- day stretch with this coach made him a pivotal figure in my life.

Every time one of my athletes calls me Coach, Charlie Janke is part of that moment because he is part of *my* mental definition of the very word Coach."

Craig: "With pride I call Coach Janke a lot of different names: A mentor who boosted me into my career as a teacher, coach and official, a leader who did anything he could to improve our sports for Michigan's athletes, a roommate at camps and clinics, an idol in the sense of how dedicated and motivated you have been to be the best coach possible to as many kids as possible, a friend who came early and stayed late at my wedding, who always found time to help me personally and professionally."

Steve: "I live in Texas now, I have seen what year-round training and great facilities can do for a team. To this day though, it still boggles my mind how student athletes from the Midwest that attended an old dilapidated school with a cinder four lane track, became one of the country's most prolific, successful cross country and track programs of a decade. It had to be the coach . . . It just had to be."

Ben: "It's truly been a blessing for me to be a part of your 45 years of coaching experience. You took a young man straight out of college with absolutely no coaching knowledge and you willingly shared every single strand of your knowledge throughout the 21 years that I have been coaching. You put equal amounts of intensity and expectations into each athlete's training regimen whether you were working with veteran athletes or newcomers.

Just about everything I do from coaching to pre-meet preparation to working with the hurdle crew, I thank you for being my example as to how things should be done."

Jeff: "A group of dedicated coaches and officials led by Charlie Janke inaugurated the first indoor track series for high schoolers in the state of Michigan in 1972.

Many of the greatest performances in Michigan prep history have occurred in these meets. The procession of talent has never let up; *future* Olympians, NCAA champions, All-Americans, not to mention future doctors, nurses, teachers and more than a few coaches, have spent many a winter's night circling the University of Michigan's track.

Never have we had more sites participate, never have we had more registered clubs, and – most importantly – never have we had so many young athletes take advantage of the opportunities. Some of them are running in the same meets their parents ran in years earlier.

None of this would be possible without the decades of volunteer work that Charlie Janke has devoted to the cause of high school track. For that, every lover of the sport in the state is indebted to Charlie."

Tony: "Chuck's love for track and field is ever present, and I'm convinced he derives his greatest pleasure from "selling" track and field and cross country to new, as well as veteran coaches."

Lou: "You have not only been a great coach and leader of young people, but you have also been an inspiration and a role model for other coaches throughout the state. For 45 years you have coached and organized with dignity and *class!*"

Rudy: "You are a wealth of information and knowledge. Your organizational skills and willingness to get a job done were obvious right from the start with the cross country state finals at Michigan International Speedway. Along with Mac, you were certainly a driving force in creating the greatest state finals in high school cross country in the nation."

Nate: "Your service and efforts with Michigan Interscholastic Track Coaches Association (MITCA) assisted this organization to be one of the premiere coaches associations in our state and nation. Your vision, organizational skills, hard work, and efforts are the reason we all enjoy, to my thinking, the best cross country finals site and format in the country.

I have been so impressed by your passion for high school/educational sport in the way you listen, in the many ways you offer help and mentor others, in the ways you respond openly and frankly, but with humility and intelligence. Your openness to others – to share your home, time and energies for meetings and gatherings resulted in better experiences for everyone involved in cross country and in track and field."

Mike: "In my 34 years of being involved in cross country and track, as an athlete and a coach, I have witnessed many changes in the sports. The one thing that has remained the same is that you would be the driving force for running in Jackson County and the state of Michigan.

Even more impressive than your outstanding record of outstanding teams and individuals is what you have given to the sports of cross country and track. While many other coaches' main concern is what is best for their team and individuals, yours has always been what lasting impact it will have on the sport."

Jeff: "I will never forget what you told me that day in a track meet. When I fell down in a hurdle race, you came running over to me, asked if I was ok, then you said, 'When you get knocked down, you get up and finish. You always finish the race.' That holds true in life and health."

Bruce: "Coach Janke's influence has been a constant with me. One of many valuable lessons I learned from Coach Janke is 'Get back up!' In a dual meet he put me in the mile run. I was a two-miler, but Coach had confidence in my abilities to earn points for the team. So the race began. In the first turn I got tangled up with another runner's feet and down I went, on the cinder track with a concrete curb. I was confused and hurt, but more importantly, on my back, as the other runners were continuing on. Through the din, I heard the distinctive voice of Coach Janke from over 50 yards away, 'GET UP! GET BACK IN THE RACE!' So that's what I did. I didn't win that race as Coach Janke had anticipated, but I did finish second.

'Get back up!' What a great lesson to learn. Life is full of adversity.

My wife and I lost our child while I was in Scotland, thousands of miles away from home.

'Get back up!'

The loss of a recommendation for advancement due to a disciplinary action while I was in the Navy.

'Get back up!'

My unexpected heart attack, with complications.

'Get back up!'

I am eternally grateful to have experienced life with Coach Janke. We don't say it enough; he will always be loved!"

In all of these snippets and stories, you can see the true joy of people who have a strong sense of purpose. Knowing who they are gives them clarity; knowing who they are created to be gives them a North Star, a focus. Purpose equips them with confidence to let go of negativity and nay-sayers. Their passion is a magnet for ideas, people and opportunities. Fortified with purpose and passion, they are empowered to take heart. They take good care of themselves, and they serve others well. They have tapped into the treasure within.

Fulfillment. They feel it.

Joy – it's deep in their souls.

Points to Ponder

1. What are your gems from the Hold Your Purpose in Your Heart chapter?

2. What are you doing to live with passion and purpose? Celebrate that!

3. What will you do to live with passion and purpose?

Jan Glowe-Janke

Chapter 19

Holding My Purpose in My Heart

I'll pick up where I left off in chapter one with the struggle. After both my parents died and I retired from education, I was exhausted. (I didn't realize it then, but I was probably grieving all the losses.) I didn't want to go anywhere, didn't want to do anything, didn't want to be around anyone. Couldn't read. Couldn't think. That is so not me. I was in a heavy dark tunnel, and I couldn't crawl out. I slept pretty much that whole first year of my retirement. To Charlie I said, "How can you stand me? I'd run away from myself if I could." Even though I was too weary to care, somehow, I knew I needed help. Usually a doctor is my last resort . . .

My doctor explained that sometimes after trauma our bodies cannot jump start themselves; she suggested a mild anti-depressant saying it's non-addictive and I could stop taking it at any time. Finally, I agreed to take an anti-depressant. It did help. I began to get back in the mainstream of life. And lily pads appeared.

Remember Sheri, the marathon runner you met in the previous chapter? And her term, lily pads, referring to people, ideas and opportunities that show up when you are acting on your passions? It happened to me too! Lily pads began to surface, one after another. And just like Sheri, my path became clear, one step at a time. (I can say that in reflection; I didn't think it or feel it so clearly at the time.)

Joining a network marketing company the year after I retired was a significant lily pad. Meeting Mickie, my first life coach, was another. Discovering my mission statement was a lily pad of epic proportions! As soon as the class with Mickie was completed, I told her, "I *have* to do what you're doing!"

She introduced me to her coach. Going through personal coaching sessions with him was the most wonderful, most awful experience ever. Wonderful because of all the learning and growing; awful because, well, growing is sometimes painful. The term "growing pains" took on a whole new meaning. (Now I know that stagnating is more painful than growing.) I began to see mindsets and patterns of behavior that were not serving me. Many of my thinking habits were getting in the way of my joy.

Let me tell you about one particular ah-ha moment that occurred in a coaching session. I was complaining about someone I care about; he was stuck, unhappy and not doing anything to change the situation. There was a long pause on the other end of the phone. I braced myself. I knew something profound was coming. My coach said, "Jan, your job is to splash love and joy, *not* to scrub – and clean – and disinfect."

Those words were like a bucket of ice water dumped over my head. It literally took my breath away. In that moment I had an epiphany. All my life, I had been trying to "fix" people. It was my default setting. As if I know what's right for them. Holy smokes! Right there I began – in earnest – to practice creating SPACE, creating a gap, to live in alignment with my mission.

How freeing to know that it's God's job to "fix" people. All I have to do (*get* to do!) is splash love and joy – on everyone. And just so you know, I am – we all are – a work in progress.

Remember our rafting trip on the Bow River (in the intro), when the wall of water shot up out of nowhere? I was about to face another wall of water that would threaten to throw me out of the boat.

The phone rang at nine o'clock on a Thursday night. Charlie had been in for a biopsy the day before, so we were waiting for a call. But at nine p.m.? I didn't even want to answer the phone. Charlie answered. The doctor told him, "You have cancer, and it's bad. Very aggressive." Charlie wasn't surprised, and he stayed calm. I was shocked – and terrified. I couldn't breathe. I cried. Charlie said gently, "No crying, Jan."

"Give me three days," I replied. I cried some. But mostly, I told friends – with his permission, sort of; I asked for prayers, and I prayed. We called people we knew who had experienced the same cancer. We researched treatment options, diligently. I was still scared, but I didn't crumble. I felt like God had prepared me. For more than a decade he had bolstered my faith through church and spiritual mentors. In my quiet times with God, I got to know him, love him and trust him. He had equipped me – I knew my purpose, and it helped me take heart. I was encouraged and strengthened by God's continual presence and help; I knew my "job." Charlie maintained his calm, optimistic attitude and ran the race set before him. I am more grateful than words can say, and relieved, to tell you that he pulled through successfully.

Once I knew my purpose, a plethora of lily pads appeared. One particular lily pad lingered in my head; it wouldn't go away. I had the idea to host a "Splash Call," a free Monday morning conference call, just 15 minutes to start the week with an uplifting message and prayer. I thought about it a lot, and I talked about it a lot. Here's a confession: Every thought about taking steps to initiate a Splash Call was accompanied by the thought, "Who am I to . . .?" and "I'm not good enough . . ."

In two different conversations on the same day, I mentioned Splash Calls to Judy and to Mickie. Both friends said, emphatically, "Jan, you've been talking about it for a year! When are you going to *do* something about it?" So, with cold, clammy hands and a knot in my throat, I went online to https://www.freeconferencecall.com, obtained a call-in number, and invited about a dozen friends. That was over ten years and 525 calls ago! (Many of the recorded calls are accessible on my Facebook page, *Splashes of Spirit*.)

About the same time I started Splash Calls, I had the idea to join Toastmasters, even though the thought of public speaking scared the daylights out of me. I admired my friends, Mickie and Anna, because they were articulate speakers. Both had been Toastmasters. I knew I needed help to be a better speaker, and especially, to grow my confidence. I looked up local Toastmasters clubs, made a call, and chickened out twice before I actually attended a meeting.

Did I have the confidence to host Splash Calls and to join Toastmasters? The answer is a resounding NO! But, I was empowered by my purpose. My mission was bigger than my fears – that's God-fidence! It's about getting myself out of his way, actually taking the step—or the leap – into the desires he had put on my heart. God-fidence is the confidence and courage to act on his Nudges and leave the outcomes to him!

I really wanted training in the spiritual component of coaching so I began searching. In a convoluted way that could only be arranged by God, I learned about Professional Christian Coaching Institute (PCCI) from a gal I didn't even know. I took their Essentials of Coaching class, and Kim Avery was one of my teachers/coaches. PCCI and Kim are lily pads – vibrant green, nourishing plants in a life-giving stream.

Kim is an example of deep faith and grace and exuberant joy; she leads by serving, generously. I wanted to copy her genius. At the time I met Kim I was overwhelmed. I knew I was called to coach but didn't know what to do first, and I didn't know *how* to do *any*thing. I decided to invest in myself by taking her Marketing Momentum class. I got traction! And focus! I developed a purpose workshop, "What on Earth Am I Here For?" and clients showed up to participate. We use the mission statement as the foundation for all follow-up coaching.

From the time I learned to tap into the treasure within, my mission statement has been imprinted on my heart. I am intentional about sparking my joy – mind, body and spirit. For me, that means letting go of mindsets and behaviors not in alignment with my mission. Letting go is like drying the wood so the joy flame can be stoked.

Habits I'm Letting Go:

> *Criticizing and second guessing myself.* After every Splash Call, I would be very frustrated with myself. I'd think of the things I should have said and things I should not have said. I knew I either had to stop the criticizing or stop the calls! So I did . . . I stopped judging every call. (We are not good "judges" of ourselves!) I leave the outcomes to God.

> *Comparing myself with others.* I have friends who do amazing work with and for the poor. Because I admire what they do, I have tried to be involved in their passion projects. But it is not where I am comfortable; nor do I feel it's where I contribute

best. My heart is not there. So I thought, "What's wrong with me? Don't I have compassion?" I have come to realize God has given *them* a heart for the poor; he has given *me* a heart to pour into those who pour into others, a heart for the elderly and for those who are grieving. That realization helps me let go of comparing myself to others (most of the time) and concentrate in areas of my strengths and passions.

> *Worrying about what others think.* Yep, it's a worry that still crosses my mind. The minute I'm aware of it, I transform it with the quote: "What others think of me is none of my business." I am grateful for my tribe; their love and appreciation feed my faith. I also stir myself up by speaking life to myself, God's words about me – I am loved, chosen and cherished. He is my audience of One, the only One I desire to please.

> *Worrying if I'm good enough.* I have to be honest, I still struggle with that – but "I don't build a condo there." I recognize it as *a thought* to take captive. It's a lie, false data, and usually I can catch it before it sinks into an emotion. Once I'm aware of that nagging thought, I pray and/or call a friend to coach me through it; and I take action. Action always makes way for confidence. And I know if God Nudges me to do something, he will make a way.

Are you getting the picture that ever since I retired, God has kept me way outside my comfort zone? He has!

I have to keep feeding my faith – every day – to starve my fears. I choose to keep my eyes on God, his purpose and the good plans he has for me.

For many years God was filling me up. For the last several years, he has been Nudging me to serve, to take action – and *share* all the magnificent lessons I'm learning – to guide others to joy!

Sharing means speaking – and that was my worst nightmare!

"Just do it!" has become my mantra. Sometimes I have to call friends so they can remind me to feel the fear and do it anyway. I make a conscious effort to shake off the fears, and I welcome every opportunity to speak. The thought of each person in my audience taking away even one gem that jazzes up their joy lights up my soul.

Ten years in Toastmasters and transformed thinking have empowered me. The butterflies are still there, but they're flying in formation! Now I embrace public speaking as a way to fulfill my mission and splash joy all around.

I've had the privilege of presenting at conferences, service clubs, women's groups, retreats and churches. The people of Morgan Park Pentecostal Church in Chicago welcomed me as their keynote speaker to celebrate their 96th anniversary – it was pure Love and joy!

Speaking is putting yourself out there – it's scary – *and* it's a confidence builder. Creating a website is also putting yourself out there, one I fearfully side-stepped for a long time. But this is the year: I hired Fresh Eyes, Inc. to create my website. This is also the year of putting myself out there by writing and publishing a book!

Ta-da!

Purpose, faith and gratitude are stepping stones that have led me to that sparkling spring inside ~ to the true joy of knowing who I am and the grand adventure of becoming who I am created to be. That's what I want for you – the true joy of being yourself.

Thank you for the privilege of allowing me to be your guide on this journey. I pray that you will tap into the treasure within, spark your joy ~ mind, body and spirit, and jazz up your joy with SPLASH habits so you can be the STAR that you are ~ and shine your light on everyone!

The world needs you to shine your light ~ as only you can do!

Jan Glowe-Janke

Part Four

Create Your Joy Plan

Jan Glowe-Janke

Chapter 20

Keys to Jump Start Your Joy

I was so excited. I was on my way to see Vickey, my best friend from high school. I hadn't seen her in decades.

It was a chilly mid-November afternoon so we planned to get a jump on Christmas shopping, and of course, talk a lot! It turned out to be an adventure that would live forever in our memories, not just for the talking and shopping.

We started at the Ann Arbor Home Goods store, and I hit the jackpot. I bought a lamp for our living room, baskets, and a beautiful comforter. We put all my purchases in the back seat of the car and drove to Briarwood Mall, a few miles down the road.

The parking lot was full. Obviously, many Christmas shoppers were getting an early start. After driving up and down a few rows, we found a spot way out by the road. We buttoned up our coats and hiked to the north entrance of the mall.

For the next three hours, we talked, snacked, talked, walked, drank coffee, shopped and talked. We covered the mall a couple times, and we covered the last several years of our lives. It was wonderful!

When we heard the announcement that the mall was closing in fifteen minutes, we began to make our way to the exit. As we talked, I absentmindedly felt around in my purse for my keys. Couldn't find them. Hmm, that was puzzling. I always put them in the same place. I checked my coat pockets. No keys. I set my purse on a counter and began to search more slowly and carefully. Still couldn't find my keys. Now I was beginning to get nervous. We were about an hour from my house, and my husband couldn't come to our rescue because he was at a coaching clinic for the weekend. I didn't have a plan for lost car keys.

We sat down in chairs near the door. Piece by piece, I took every item out of my purse and put it in my lap. Still no keys. We backtracked. We re-visited all the stores we'd been in, checked at desks where we had made purchases and talked to clerks to ask if anyone had turned in keys. Still no keys. And still no plan. Who would I call for help? How would we get home? Having no idea of what to do heightened my anxiety.

Revived Hope

Vickey said, "Maybe you dropped them on the ground when you got out of the car." With revived hope, we gathered our packages and walked outside. As we got close enough to see my car, I thought aloud, "That's strange, the dashboard lights are on . . ."

Simultaneously, Vickey and I realized that not only were the lights on, *my car was still running*! My keys were in the ignition! *And* I'd left the car unlocked with $400 worth of my Home Goods purchases in plain view in the back seat!

We looked at each other in shock for a second, then we burst out in laughter – loud, uncontrollable peals of laughter that pierced the darkness. To say I am embarrassed is an understatement! However, there is some comfort in knowing I'm not the only one. You've lost your keys too, haven't you? But you probably didn't leave them in the ignition with the car running!

🐾🐾🐾🐾🐾🐾🐾

Our joy can be as elusive as keys. Sometimes we misplace those little buggers, for a few minutes, an hour, or more. Just like keys, our joy can easily get lost, lost in the busy-ness of day-to-day responsibilities, lost in the trials, storms and the rough waters we encounter. That's understandable. And that's normal. But we don't have to "build a condo there." We don't have to stay joy-less.

When I couldn't find my keys, and I didn't have a plan for how to get home, I was very anxious. My anxiety and frustration increased by the minute, and it was sucking the joy out of fun with my friend. A plan for lost keys would have made a world of difference.

Just like my keys were right there, our joy is right there, within our grasp. Our joy is always present; it's *inside us*. We just need to know how to get at it and make a conscious effort to connect to it. It's about getting home to our joy.

The good news is: We *can* be prepared. We can make *a plan.* So when joy thieves show up, we're not thrown into a tizzy; we can keep CALM and enjoy the ride. We can cross our arms over our chests, put our feet out in front of us and stay in the flow, in the fun!

Create Your JOY PLAN

You've "gotta wanna" – so get that desire for joy in your head and heart. It's a part of the treasure within you, and it's your responsibility to connect to that joy.

> ***Identify what joy is for you***
> ***– this is essential.***

Think about it, write about it and talk about it. The more clear you are about what you want, the more likely it is to happen.

Joy Plan Framework

This is not intended to be a checklist; think of it as a framework from which to select the keys that will jump start your joy. Choose the ones that resonate with you. The Joy Plan Framework is available for download on my website, https://janjanke.com.

Consider developing two different plans.

1. *Create your personalized joy plan.* Decide what you will do daily, weekly and/or monthly. For example, I am intentional about reading devotionals, exercise, connecting with friends, speaking positively and practicing gratitude.

2. *Create your go-to plan* for times when rough waters threaten to throw you out of the boat. For example, in tough times I meditate on my mission statement, call a close friend and pray.

Chapter 1 – Your Purpose
- Write the truths about you
- Identify what drives your life

Chapter 2 – Discover Your Purpose – A Guide
- Do the 7-Step Guide to discover your purpose
- Hire a life coach
- Read *The Path*

Chapter 3 – Stay CALM
- Control thoughts you focus on
- Adapt to your situation
- Limit the news
- Meditate

Chapter 4 – Relax
- Unplug
- Sit spot
- Rest hour
- Breath practices
- Sleep routine

Chapter 5 – Refresh

- Move
- Socially connect
- Spend time in nature
- Volunteer

Chapter 6 – Renew

- Restore something
- Transform a mindset

Chapter 7 – Create SPACE

- Identify situations that cause stress
- Identify healthy thoughts and responses
- Create space to practice healthy responses

Chapter 8 – Be the STAR that You Are

- Read the poem just for fun
- Read the poem with someone fun

Chapter 9 – Let Go

- Identify a worry or fear to let go
- Turn a worry into a prayer
- Say a thank-you-ahead-of-time prayer

Chapter 10 – Shake It Off

- Think of your biggest worry
- Have a shake it off session
- Have a shake it off party!

Chapter 11 – Feed Your Faith

- Read/Listen
- Sing/Praise
- Pray (ACTS)
- Ask someone to mentor you
- Think/Write about what you want
- Good Day Practice (Journal)

Chapter 12 – Celebrate Resilience

- Accept
- Forgive
- What is one decision that could make this your best year ever?
- Look for the closed doors and open windows in your life
- Meet monthly with a group of supportive friends
- Study successful people
- Find a way

Chapter 13 – Smile

- Smile on purpose
- Start a smile file

Chapter 14 – Play

- Play 5-10 minutes each day
- Schedule a fun activity each month

Chapter 15 – Laugh

- Make a date with someone who makes you laugh
- Keep a journal of funny things people say/do.

Chapter 16 – Appreciate

- Keep a gratitude journal
- Speak words of appreciation to someone
- Write a handwritten note to a person you appreciate

Chapter 17 – Speak Life

- Choose an affirmation to say to yourself
- Say kind, complimentary words to someone
- Speak positively about a difficult situation
- Choose a Scripture to declare

Chapter 18 – Hold Your Purpose in Your Heart

- Write your purpose; put it where you see it
- Speak your purpose to yourself, daily
- Tell a friend your purpose

❦❦❦❦❦❦❦

In this book you've learned to tap into the treasure within. You have learned to spark your joy ~ mind, body and spirit. You've learned SPLASH habits to jazz up your joy.

All the tapping, sparking and jazzing train your brain to be positive. Now you are equipped with a whole suitcase of keys to take you home to your joy.

I am doing cartwheels for you because you are taking responsibility for your joy!

Gratitude

"The root of joy is gratefulness.
It is not joy that makes us grateful;
It is gratitude that makes us joyful."
Brother David Steindl-Rast

I am overflowing with gratitude, and I'm saying so!
My heart is filled with joy!

Thank you, God!
For lavishing love on me, drawing my heart to yours and leading me in your way. Thank you for teaching me to trust your timing; delay is not denial! Thank you for the gift of each person you have loaned to me – for a reason, a season or a lifetime – for your grace and theirs as I lean into becoming the joy-splasher you created me to be.

Thank you to my teachers, coaches and friends who have helped me find my God-given purpose, my God-fidence, my voice, and for showing me the way forward.
Mickie Zada, Frank Mallinder, Kim Avery, Chris McCluskey, Sheila Fitzgerald, Pastor Ron Martoia, Maureen Zappala, Kyle Maurer, Craig Carrel and Sam Horn.

Thank you to my friends who responded so thoughtfully to my joy survey.

You expanded and deepened my thinking about joy. You wrote that you wanted to hear how real people deal with real-life struggles and still manage to be joyful. I took your desire to heart, and it became a guiding light for this book.

Thank you to all my Toastmasters friends.

A decade of weekly meetings, learning about you, learning from you was delightful! Thank you for providing an incredibly supportive environment; it was the perfect place to practice making the butterflies in my stomach fly in formation. If many sections of this book sound familiar, it's because you heard them first as my speeches!

Thank you to all my Splash Call friends.

You show up on the phone every Monday morning, and your sweet voices bring joy to my heart! It's glorious to start our week together – rejoicing in the Light of God's Love!

Thank you to each of my coaching clients.

The work of discovering your God-given purpose puts us on holy ground, and it brings deep joy to my soul. I am eternally grateful that you trust me with your heart. *Thank you for permission to share your beautiful mission statements:* Kelly Kluver, Kim Foreman, Rebecca Miller, Glenn DiBartolomeo, Mandie Kolkman, Jeanette Lamphere, Shannon Diffenderffer,

Becky Clark, Dan Nelson, Kathy Howard, Janet Hanson, TJ Bolt, and Sheri Bush.

Thank you to my friends who wrote sections of my book.
Sue and Todd Gabrielson, Jeanette Lamphere, Julie Matteson Warfield, Laura Coffey, Michelle Cochran, Mary Collver and Cherie Fish.

Thank you to each friend and family member who allowed me to write about you.
Melissa Balogh Waidley, Mark Corless, Mickie Zada, TJ Bolt, Sheri Bush, Jennifer Robinson, Karolyn Karl, Kim Glowe, Katy Glowe, Craig Carrel, Bill Lundberg, Sheri Peterson, Kathy Meister, Tim Prueter, Vickey Sabin, Linda Whitney, Bert and Vickie Steck, Tim and Susie Swedine, Robin Steely, Wendy Huff and more.

Thank you to our friends who see and appreciate Charlie's passion, and said so!
Jim Martin, Mark Devereau, Sarah Braunreiter Ryan, Corey Pryor, Josh Keagle, Sheri Chatters Peterson, Beth Ann Lannen Walz, Aretha Davis, Lezlie Crossley, Herb Fitzer, Craig Vitale, Steve Banovic, Ben Thomas, Jeff Hollogaugh, Toni Magni, Lou Miramonti, Rudy Godefroidt, Nate Hampton, Mike Woolsey, Jeff Krum, Bruce Petosky and more.

Thank you to my dear ones for your continual love, encouragement, support and prayers. For years, you have been the wind beneath my wings.
Jennifer, Brad, Zac and Jake Robinson, Judy Bartel, Mary Collver, Nancy Wilson, Karolyn Karl, Delores Kingsbury, Cherie Fish, TJ Bolt, Sandra Harkness, Jill

Geers, Wendy Huff, Shannon Diffenderffer, Tamra Stier, Pam Watts, Susan Howard, Lindy Crandell and more.

Prayer Group Gals, thank you for the privilege of coaching a group purpose workshop with you; I am still in awe of the Holy Spirit's dance among us! Thanks too for showing me "Jesus with skin on" and for your powerful prayers.

Jeanette Lamphere, Laura Coffey, Julie Matteson Warfield, Leigh MacCready, Pat Timmons, Karen Hulett, Dawn Williams, Sue Leece, Janet Hanson, Becky Cartwright and Melissa Balogh Waidley.

Thank you to my family, friends and former students not listed by name.

Please know you have touched my heart, you have enriched my life, and you are precious to me.

Book Angels

Sue Gabrielson

You have poured yourself into editing this book as passionately as if it was your own, and your wholehearted enthusiasm makes my heart sing. Together we mulled over every idea, every word. You listened to me – a lot! You asked thought-full, thought-provoking questions, tactfully, and taught me so much. You smoothed out wrinkles in my thinking and in my soul. Collaborating with you restored my joy in writing this book. Without you, Sue, this book and my sanity simply would not/could not be! You are an editor extraordinaire and a generous, gracious friend.

Mark Corless

Your intuitive coaching on every chapter of this book fired me up! Your wisdom was like a kaleidoscope that brought depth and dimension to my thinking. I am deeply grateful for all the time and energy you dedicated to reviewing my writing, and I treasure your friendship more than words can say.

Sam Horn

Heartfelt thanks for the generous gift of *So, You Want to Write a Book*. Your inspiring and practical program taught every detail about book writing and publishing – You equipped me!

Mason Harris

You bravely answered my plea for an accountability partner, and you turned out to be a fabulous book-writing buddy and friend. Thank you for keeping me anchored, encouraged, and moving forward. I can't wait to read *your* book, *The Chutzpah Advantage*!

Kim Foreman

You designed the most beautiful book cover ever – *I love it!* You really do work magic, Kim, and I am filled with awe and gratitude. MWAH!

Michele Wilson

Cover photo credit to you – along with my heartfelt thanks for capturing the Spirit of Joy!

Susan Bliss Pearce

You are the first author in our family! Thank you for your inspiring example, for your encouragement all along the way and for introducing me to . . .

Intellect Publishing, LLC & John O'Melveny Woods

Thank you for your commitment to making this book everything I wanted and for making *Splashes of Spirit ~ A Guide to Joy* a reality.

And Charlie

I am so grateful to you and for you. Thank you for loving me unconditionally, for your enthusiasm about this book and for always being my rock! I'm still crazy about you!

Notes

1. Shawn Achor, 2011. "The Happiness Advantage: Linking Positive Brains to Performance." Bloomington, TEDx, (12:29).
https://www.youtube.com/watch?v=GXy__kBVq1M

2. Christine Carter, "Finding Happiness and Meaning at Work and at Home." You Tube Video, 3:29. Nov. 15, 2016.
https://www.youtube.com/watch?v=cYeJkNcioIA

3. Dr. Michael Edwards is CEO of The Schuster Center which is the Business School for Dentists and the author of *Through the Red Sea: A Path to Private Care* and *Are You Essential?*

4. Rick Warren, *The Purpose-Driven Life: What on Earth Am I Here For?* (Grand Rapids, MI: Zondervan, 2002), 27.

5. Warren, *The Purpose-Driven Life*, 30.

6. Patty Onderko, "The Science of Being Happy: Simple Suggestions for Loving Your Life," *Success*, August, 2014, 53.

7. Max McKeown, Wikipedia, last edited July 20, 2019,
https://en.wikipedia.org/wiki/Max_McKeown. (I use a variation of McKeown's 4 levels of adaptability.)

8. Jeff Boss, "14 Signs of an Adaptable Person," *Forbes*, September 3, 2015.

9. Mayo Clinic Staff, "Relaxation Techniques: Try These Steps to Reduce Stress," *Healthy Lifestyle*, April 18, 2020.
https://www.mayoclinic.org/healthy-lifestyle/stress-management/in-depth/relaxation-technique/art-20045368

10. Sheri's website: https://www.yourpathcoach.org

11. Cleveland Clinic, "Here's What Happens When You Don't Get Enough Sleep," *Health Essentials*, June 16, 2020.
https://health.clevelandclinic.org/happens-body-dont-get-enough-sleep/

12. Parker Palmer, "Down is the Way to Well-Being," *Spirituality & Health*, July/August, 2018, 24, 25. [Excerpt from Parker Palmer's *On the Brink of Everything: Grace, Gravity & Getting Old*, CA: Berrett-Koehler Publishers, Inc.]

13. Joyce Meyer, "life point," *The Everyday Life Bible, Amplified Version*, (NY: Faith Words), 1086.

14. Bill Hybels with LaVonne Neff, *Too Busy Not to Pray*; 2nd ed., (IL: InterVarsity Press, 1998), 62-73.

15. Sarah Stevenson, "There's Magic in Your Smile," *Psychology Today*, June 25, 2012.

16. Susan Barry, "I Feel Your Smile, I Feel Your Pain," *Psychology Today*, February 7, 2011.

17. Jennifer Wallace, "Why It's Good for Grownups to Go Play," *Washington Post*, May 20, 2017.

18. Stuart Brown, *Play, How It Shapes the Brain, Opens the Imagination, and Invigorates the Soul.* (NY: Avery, 2009), 7.

19. Christopher McCluskey, interview with Susan Whitcomb, "Gratitude: The Hidden Benefits of Thankfulness," Professional Christian Coaching Today podcast audio, Nov. 24, 2015. https://professionalchristiancoaching.com/008- gratitude-the-hidden-benefits-of-thankfulness-with-susan-whitcomb-pcc/

20. Patty Onderko, "The Science of Being Happy," *Success*, August, 2014. [On page 52 she refers to Rick Hanson's book, *Hardwiring Happiness: The New Brain Science of Contentment, Calm and Confidence.*]

Dive into Splash Calls

Splash Calls are about starting your week in the light of God's love rather than with your to-do list. The uplifting thoughts, stories, Scripture and prayers will feed your faith so treat yourself to these fun, interactive conference calls.

Links to the following recorded calls are available at https://janjanke.com ~ Enjoy!

#265 – Thank You, God; I Know that Was You! and Mickie's Happy-Ever-After Story (18:00)

#313 – Lose the Inner Critic (15:00)

#420 – The Good Day Practice (20:00)

#426 – Grateful and Saying So (18:30)

#496 – Stay CALM (19:30)

#517 – Feed Your Faith and Sit Spot (19:10)

Visit Facebook page – *Splashes of Spirit* – for links to more recorded calls.

Jan Glowe-Janke

About the Author

Jan is a joy coach and a gifted speaker who delivers inspiring, fun, interactive messages that guide people to their joy.

She began her professional journey following her passion to teach and went on to earn master's degrees in education and in school counseling. Since retiring from public school education, Jan's classroom has expanded. She developed a mission-statement writing workshop and has been coaching people to discover their God-given purpose since 1999.

Jan lives in Brooklyn, Michigan, with her husband Charlie where she continues to learn and grow and enjoy the process of becoming who God created her to be – a joy splasher!

You may contact Jan about:

o *Speaking* at your *Splashes of Spirit, A Guide to Joy* book study group

- o *Speaking* at your event or with your group
- o *Coaching* to discover and write your mission statement

You may connect with Jan at:

- o https://janjanke.com
- o Facebook page -- *Splashes of Spirit*

Made in the USA
Monee, IL
17 April 2021